PRAYER STORM

DAILY PRAYER GUIDE

SUPERNATURAL RESULTS

NOVEMBER – DECEMBER 2025

Godson T. Nembo

CRNPUBLICATIONS   IEM PRESS

SUPERNATURAL DOCUMENTS

Copyright @ October 2025

Published in Cameroon by:
Christian Restoration Network
crnprayerstorm@gmail.com,
prayerstorm@christianrestorationnetwork.org

ISBN: 978-1-63603-331-0

CONTACT
P.O. Box 31339 Biyem-assi, Yaounde, Cameroon
Tel.: 679.46.57.17, 652.38.26.93 or 696.56.58.64
Email: **godsonnembo@gmail.com** or
contact@christianrestorationnetwork.org
www.christianrestorationnetwork.org

WHERE TO BUY THIS PRAYER GUIDE:
SEE THE LAST PAGE

YOU CAN ACCESS ALL PRINTED HARD COPIES OF OUR BOOKS FOR ANY SPECIFIED DURATION AT YOUR DOORSTEP.
Contact (237) 679465717 for subscription and payment details.

Prayer Storm Online Store: With MTN or Orange Mobile Money *(for those in Cameroon)* and E-Wallet *(for those abroad)*, you can easily obtain the electronic version of this book and other CRN publications via **www.amazon.com** at **https://shorturl.at/pqxyT** or **www.christianrestorationnetwork.org/our-bookstore** or **https://goo.gl/ktf3rT**

Printed in Yaounde, Cameroon by Mama press: (237) 677581523

TESTIMONIES:
Your testimony is a weapon against the kingdom of darkness. It is also a seed for someone else's miracle. Share with us what God has used this prayer guide and our books to do in your life; by SMS, telephone call or email.

BECOME A MINISTRY PARTNER:
Call the numbers: (237) 679.46.57.17 or 652.38.26.93 or 696.56.58.64 or send an email to:
crnprayerstorm@gmail.com or
contact@christianrestorationnetwork.org

iii

Send your financial seed to:

- ECOBANK Acc. Nº: **0040812604565101**
- Carmel Cooperative Credit Union Ltd. Bamenda Acc. Nº: **261**
- ORANGE Mobile Money Acc. Nº: **699902618**
- MTN Mobile Money Acc. Nº: **674495895**

A NEED FOR DISTRIBUTORS:

If you are interested in the distribution of this Prayer Storm Daily Prayer Guide, call or send an SMS to any of these numbers for negotiations: (237) 675.68.60.05 or 677.43.69.64 or 652.38.26.93 or 696.56.58.64 or send an email to: **crnprayerstorm@gmail.com** (see last page).

TABLE OF CONTENTS

IMPORTANT EVENTS/ANNOUNCEMENTS

SPECIAL PRAYER STORM PROGRAM

5 NIGHTS OF POWER WITH PASTOR GODSON	Theme	Date	Join us
	SUPERNA TURAL RESULTS	*From Monday 1st to Friday 5th December 2025*	daily at midnight (GMT +1) on Zoom, Facebook, YouTube.

SPECIAL PROGRAM: I PRAY FOR YOU

Join Pastor Godson for a half hour morning devotion
every **MONDAY, WEDNESDAY, and FRIDAY**
from **6am** live on Facebook, YouTube
@PastorGodsonNemboTangumonkem

HOUR OF RESTORATION

Join Pastor Godson & Anna TANGUMONKEM for
HOUR OF RESTORATION every **TUESDAY**
morning from **6 – 7:30am** in the banquet hall: Salle des
fêtes « Fontaine de grâce » at Jouvence, Mendong street
– Yaounde, Cameroon..
A time of prophetic intercession for individuals, families and the nations.

ANNOUNCEMENTS

➢ Festival of Fire series No. 1-5 and Power Must Change Hands Vol. 1-10 now available at XAF 3,000. Send your orders from today.

- ➤ Annual subscription to the Daily Prayer Guide from XAF 10,000 for electronic copies.
- ➤ All our books are available at our CRN Head office: 1st Floor Storey Building at Entrée Lycée de Tsinga village on the edge of the main road. **Contact:** 681.72.24.04, 695.72.23.40
- ➤ Carmel Credit Union, Yaoundé branch located at Carrefour Biyem-Assi, on the ground floor of the storey building, opposite Campus Crusade for Christ. **Contact:** +237 652.83.55.04
- ➤ Prayer Storm Bookshop at Cow Street Nkwen – Bamenda sells our books, Bibles and excellent Christian literature. **Contact:** 675.14.04.50, 674.59.35.98, 679.46.57.17.

"RESTORATION CAMP" Project

- • The project for the establishment of the base for CRN in Yaounde, Cameroon began in January 2020.
- • The LAYING OF THE FOUNDATION STONE FOR THE RESTORATION PRAYER HOUSE at Tsinga Village, Yaounde, took place in December 2023.
- • For information on how to be part of the project, call or send SMS to **(237) 674.49.58.95, 678.16.46.88, 673.50.42.33, 699.90.26.18.**

Feedback Questionnaire:

We will love to hear your suggestions on how we can improve on this book: Send your comments to **(237) 681722404**, use the link https://prayer-stormdevotional.paperform.com/ or scan the QR CODE shown here to fill the online form.

HOW TO BECOME A CHILD OF GOD

Going to church and praying is not enough. *"Except a man is BORN AGAIN, he CANNOT SEE the kingdom of God." (John 3:3).*

The following steps will help you know how you can be born again.

Step 1: God Loves You and Offers a Wonderful Plan for Your Life

"For God so loved the world that He gave His only begotten Son, that whoever believes in Him should not perish but have everlasting life" (John 3:16). Jesus said, *"I came that they might have life and have it to the full." (John 10:10).*

No matter who you are and what you have done, God still loves you and wants to save you (Rom.5:8).

Step 2: Your Sins Have Separated You from God; That Is Why You Are Not Experiencing His Wonderful Plan for Your Life

"For all have sinned and fall short of the glory of God" (Rom.3:23)
"The wages of sin is death (spiritual separation from God) Rom.6:23.

All your religious activities and efforts cannot save you. God has provided a solution for you.

Step 3: Jesus Christ Is the Only Way Back to God

Jesus said, *"I am the way, the truth and the life, No one comes to the father except through me" (John 14:6).* Jesus is the only sacrifice God can accept for your sins. Through Him you can connect to God's plan for your life.

Step 4: You Must Personally Receive Jesus Christ as Your Saviour and Lord. Then You Can Know and Experience God's Plan for Your Life

Receive Him by personal invitation and by faith. *"Behold, I stand at the door and knock. If anyone hears My voice and opens the door (your heart), I will come in to him and dine with him, and he with Me." (Rev.3:20).*

If you are ready now to give your life to Jesus Christ, pray this prayer with all your heart.

"Dear Lord Jesus Christ, I need you. I open the door of my life and receive you as my Saviour and Lord. Forgive all my sins and wash me with your blood. Make me the kind of person you want me to be. Thank you for saving me."

Congrats! You are now a child of God.

Call us now let us pray for you: (237) 652.38.26.93 or 696.56.58.64

(Pastor Godson T. Nembo & Prayer Storm Team)

NOW THAT YOU ARE BORN AGAIN

Making the decision to become a born-again Christian, is the best decision you've ever made in your entire life and I congratulate you for that. The following points will help you enjoy your newfound life in Christ Jesus.

1. **Live with the Consciousness that You are Saved:** It is fundamental that you are certain of your new faith. This is referred to as the Assurance of Salvation. Believe that your sins have been forgiven and forgotten by God because of the price Jesus paid by His sacrificial death on the cross and that you are no longer under any condemnation (Acts 16:31, Rom.8:1-2, 2Cor.5:17, Jn.1:12).

2. **Join a Fellowship:** By new birth, you have entered the family of God. Locate a church that teaches and practises the scriptures truthfully, where the worship enables you to encounter God, and where the people are friendly and spiritual growth is encouraged (Heb.10:25, Gal.6:10).

3. **Get a Bible and Study It Daily:** You can begin from John, then Acts, Romans, etc. Just as a baby needs physical nourishment in order to grow, the Word of God is also the spiritual food by which we grow into Christlikeness (1Pet.2:2, Jn.5:24). Consult other mature Christians for any explanations.

4. **Commune Daily with God:** Through prayer, we talk with God, express our burdens to Him, as well as offer worship, praise and appreciation. We also have the privilege to get God speak to us, showering upon us His

love, peace, blessings and divine direction (Rom.10:9, 1Thess.5:17, 1Pet.5:8).

5. **Destroy Satan's Property in Your Keeping:** Desist from anything that does not glorify God. Do away with anything evil related to your sinful past, such as pornographic materials, stolen money and possessions, talismans, charms, juju, etc. (2Cor.6:17, Tit.2:11).

6. **Separate from Evil Friends and Get New Godly Friends:** Now that you are born again, you must discontinue the former way of life and walk in the truth (Ps.1:1-3, 2Cor.4:2; 5:17, Eph.4:22, 1Jn.1:6).

7. **Get Baptized:** Water baptism by immersion publicly authenticates our salvation and affirms our membership in the body of Christ (Rom.6:4, Col.2:12, Matt.28:19, Acts 2:38, 8:36).

8. **Seek the Baptism of the Holy Spirit:** The Holy Spirit assures us that we are saved and empowers us to live a holy life and do exploits for God through special gifts (Rom.8:14, Acts 2:1-4; 10:38, Eph.5:18).

9. **Tell Others about Jesus:** Our character should testify about our inner transformation. Also, our eagerness to tell others about God's love and lead them to Christ is also evidential about our salvation (Jn.4:28-29, Acts 4:10; 22:14, 2Tim.2:2).

10. **Worship God with Your Wealth through Offerings and Tithes:** Our cheerful giving is essential in advancing God's Kingdom – freewill offerings and tithe (one-tenth

of our increase) (Deut.16:16-17, Prov.3:9-10, 2Cor:9:7).

11. **Make the Life of Christ Your Standard:** Fix your eyes on Jesus, the Author and Finisher of our faith Make Him your Role Model (Heb.12:2, Phil.2:5-11, Eph.4:24).

12. **Don't Abandon; Rise and Continue, if you Fall:** The Christian race may seem tough and challenging, with persecutions, distractions, oppositions, and even discouragements. But rest assured, you will make it by faith (Prov.24:16, Isa.41:10, Phil.1:6).

I pray that you will stand firm, and finish well like other heroes of faith, in Jesus' name! Amen.

Call us for counselling and prayer: (237) 652.38.26.93 or 696.56.58.64.

(Pastor Godson T. Nembo & Prayer Storm Team)

HOW TO USE THIS DAILY PRAYER GUIDE

I have discovered that some people do not know how to use this book well. As a result, they are not benefiting much from it. I will like to explain to you, how you can either use it during your personal prayer time or how to use it to lead a group prayer session.

Your Personal Prayer Time:

1. ***Read the topic of the day:*** It is the summary of the message of the day.
2. ***Read the Bible passages of the day aloud:*** You retain more, when you read aloud to yourself. In the early days, scriptures were read aloud.
3. ***Read the meditation slowly:*** Do it with a strong desire to understand.
4. ***Pray the prayer points:*** Read each prayer point and take time to pray well before you read the next one.
5. ***Pray for others:*** Use the prayer point to pray for other people as inspired by the Holy Spirit.
6. ***Add other prayer topics:*** For instance; dedicate your day, your family, your job, your Church, etc. to God.
7. Pray for your specific needs and those of others.
8. ***Prophetic Prayers of the Week:*** These prayers will be brought up every Monday. We encourage you to pray them every day during the week that follows.

Leading a Group to Pray:

1. Read the topic of the day aloud.
2. Assign one or more persons to read the Bible passage of the day aloud.
3. Read the meditation of the day aloud. After reading, you

can make some comments, if necessary.

4. Allow other members of the group to make contributions or ask questions, if they have them.

5. Read one prayer point at a time. Then allow the people to pray for some time before you read the next one.

6. After they have prayed in chorus, you can ask one person to raise his/her voice and pray.

7. When you finish reading the prayer points, first ask the group members to give their own personal prayer plan.

8. At the end, let one person pray and conclude the session.

Bible Reading Plan:

We have included two Bible reading plans: **"Bible in 1 year"** and **"Bible in 2 years."** You can read through your Bible in one year by following the first plan in two years by following the second plan. Set aside time every day to read your Bible.

Saturday 1 November　　　**CONSECRATED AND ANOINTED**

Read: Numbers 7:1

Bible in 1 year: 2 & 3 John, Jude
Bible in 2 years: Dan 8-9

"You have loved righteousness and hated lawlessness; therefore God, Your God, has anointed You with the oil of gladness more than Your companions" (Hebrews 1:9 NKJV).

The fundamental key to the anointing God wants to release on you is consecration. In fact, the pattern of Scripture is clear: consecration always precedes anointing. Just as vessels are cleaned before oil is poured into them, God purifies His servants before releasing His Spirit upon them.

In Numbers 7, Moses consecrated and anointed inanimate objects for God's service, underscoring the importance of this principle. If lifeless objects required consecration before use, how much more must we, the living temples of God, be cleansed and set apart for His purposes?

Similarly, the priests in the Old Testament went through a strict process before ministry. They were washed with water, clothed in holy garments, purified with sacrificial blood, and finally anointed with oil (Leviticus 8). This pointed to the deeper truth that holiness precedes power.

The New Testament reveals this pattern in the life of Christ. Hebrews 1:9 tells us Jesus was anointed above His companions because He loved righteousness and hated wickedness. His consecration qualified Him for the fullness of the Spirit's anointing.

Today, many desire power without purity, influence without intimacy, and anointing without consecration. But God does not anoint unclean vessels (2 Timothy 2:21). Likewise, when an anointed person loses consecration, the oil dries up and ministry becomes empty. If you want the anointing, stay away from sin.

Let us therefore pursue holiness, not as a religious duty, but as the joyful surrender of a vessel that longs to carry the oil of heaven. The deeper the consecration, the richer the anointing.

Let us pray

1. *Father, thank You for cleansing me through the blood of Jesus and setting me apart as Your vessel.*
2. *Father, set me free from every form of compromise and impurity, in Jesus' name.*
3. *Lord Jesus, help me to love righteousness and hate wickedness like You did.*
4. *Father, let Your anointing flow fresh in my life as I walk in consecration, in Jesus' name.*
5. *Father, as You give me gifts, transform me into a holy vessel, in Jesus' name.*
6. *I am a clean vessel, anointed mighty for supernatural results, in Jesus' name.*

Sunday 2 November   **ANOINTED FOR UNCOMMON RESULTS**

Read: 1 Samuel 16:1-13

Bible in 1 year: Zech. 1-3
Bible in 2 years: Dan 10-11:1-22

"Then Samuel took the horn of oil and anointed him in the midst of his brothers; and the Spirit of the Lord came upon David from that day forward" (1 Samuel 16:13).

The anointing empowers the believer for uncommon results. When the prophet Samuel poured oil on David's head, he was still a young shepherd in the fields. Outwardly, nothing seemed to change. But inwardly, everything shifted. The Spirit of the Lord came upon him. The anointing marked him for destiny. From that day forward, David carried divine empowerment for uncommon results.

The word anoint comes from the Hebrew *'Mashach'*, meaning to smear, consecrate, or set apart for a purpose. In the New Testament, Jesus is called the Christ, from the Greek "Christos", meaning the Anointed One. This shows that true anointing is found in Jesus Christ Himself. When we are in Him, His Spirit rests on us, equipping us beyond natural limits.

David didn't have to fight for the throne; the oil fought for him. Goliath, political storms, and rejection could not stop him because the anointing made him more than a conqueror.

Likewise, the Spirit of Christ will enable you to achieve results beyond human imagination. Your talent may open doors, but only the anointing sustains influence with eternal impact. Think of electricity flowing into a light bulb. Without the current, the bulb is just glass and wire – ordinary and lifeless. But when power flows through it, the bulb shines brightly, transforming the environment. In the same way, you may look ordinary, but when Christ's anointing flows through you, you illuminate the world with uncommon results.

Are you struggling to accomplish a spiritual assignment with human strength? You need the anointing. Little will become much, your weakness will turn into strength, and fear into courage. The anointing transforms shepherds into kings, fishermen into apostles, and sinners into saints.

Stay connected to Jesus, the Source of the oil. The anointing flows in intimacy with Him. You are not average; you are anointed in Christ for divine impact.

Let us pray

1. *Father, I thank You for Your anointing coming on me afresh today, in Jesus' name.*
2. *Father, let fresh oil be poured upon my life today for supernatural results, in Jesus' name.*
3. *O Lord, stir up every spiritual gift and calling sleeping within me, in Jesus' name.*
4. *Father, let Your anointing empower me to overcome every giant opposing my destiny, in Jesus' name.*
5. *Father, cause Your anointing upon my life to produce undeniable results, in Jesus' name.*

6. *I am anointed by the oil of the Holy Spirit; I will see uncommon results this month, in Jesus' name.*

Monday 3 November　　　　**SUPERNATURAL OPEN DOORS**

Read: Isaiah 45:1-5

> **Bible in 1 year:** Zech. 4-6
> **Bible in 2 years:** Dan 11:23-45; 12

"See, I have placed before you an open door that no one can shut" (Revelation 3:8b NIV).

S upernatural open doors attract uncommon favor in a believer's life. This is what God is about to do in your life.

When God opens a door, no one, no system, or demons can shut it. Why? Nothing can challenge God's authority. If He says yes in your life, no one can say no. When He blesses you, no one can curse you (Numbers 23:8).

Supernatural results often begin with divine access or opportunities that your strength could never secure. Supernatural doors are opened by favor, not force. Esther was an orphan in a foreign land, but when her moment came, *"she won the favor of everyone who saw her" (Esther 2:15)*. I don't think Esther was more physically beautiful than all the other girls. The uncommon favor on her opened the king's heart to marry her and save her people, Israel.

Revelation 3:7-8 reminds us that Jesus holds the key of David. He opens doors no one can shut, and shuts what no one can open. This is divine positioning: you don't manipulate your way in; God ushers you in. You have to trust Him.

Isaiah 45 reveals that God can go before you to level mountains, break gates of bronze, and give you treasures hidden in darkness. These are doors you didn't knock. He opened them because you obeyed Him.

Are you going through a situation where you feel like every door is locked? Remember this: Jesus has the Master Key. Stay faithful to Him. Stay humble, and be sensitive to His timing.

Favor isn't luck. It's divine access. God will open one door this season and change everything.

Let us pray

1. *Father, thank You because You have the key to open every door I need, in Jesus' name.*
2. *Father, position me this season for divine opportunities and open doors I could never access by myself, in Jesus' name.*
3. *I command every barrier, gate, or resistance standing against my family's advancement to break, in Jesus' name.*
4. *Father, clothe me with uncommon favor like You did for Esther, in Jesus' name.*
5. *Father, reveal and unlock hidden treasures and relationships assigned to my destiny, in Jesus' name.*
6. *I declare: Doors are opening for my family and me that no one can shut; we will walk in uncommon favor, in Jesus' name.*

Prophetic Prayers of the Week

1. *"And they overcame him by the blood" (Rev. 12:11); By the blood of Jesus, I overcome every accusation, battle, and enemy this month, and I am unshakable, in Jesus' name.*
2. *"With God all things are possible"* (Matt. 19:26); *Impossible situations bow to results, in Jesus' name.*

3. *"The Lord will make a way in the wilderness"* (Isa. 43:19); *My wilderness turns to a testimony this month, in Jesus' name.*

Tuesday 4 November   FAITH UNLOCKS
                          THE IMPOSSIBLE

Read: Mark 11:22-24;
         Hebrews 11:1-6

Bible in 1 year: Zech. 7-10
Bible in 2 years: Rev. 1-2

"With God nothing shall be impossible" (Luke 1:37).

G od specializes in the impossible. We call Him "The impossibility specialist." What man cannot do, God can, through our faith. Faith is not just belief; it is the confident, obedient response to what God has said/promised, even when circumstances contradict it.

When the angel visited Mary, he spoke an impossible word: *"You will conceive... though you are a virgin."* Mary's response was simple but powerful: *"Be it unto me according to your word" (Luke 1:38).* That was the faith that unlocked the supernatural.

In Mark 11:22-24, Jesus taught that faith can move impossible mountains. Not just small problems; but massive, immovable barriers. Hebrews 11 lists men and women who received what was promised, conquered kingdoms, and shut the mouths of lions, not by strength, but by faith.

What impossible thing are you facing in your family? A diagnosis? A delay? A dream that seems unreachable? Faith doesn't deny the facts; it refuses to be limited by them. It looks beyond the natural and anchors itself in the unchanging Word of God.

I remember a woman who came to one of our programs sick. She had just returned from the hospital,

29

where she was diagnosed with cancer in her leg. The doctors requested 800,000 FCFA ($1,500) to begin her treatment. She didn't have the money. She came to the altar trusting God for a miracle. After that program, the cancer on her leg disappeared completely.

If God has spoken, believe, declare, and act. Faith not only pleases God; it gives Him room to move.

The supernatural is unlocked when faith rises above fear.

Let us pray

1. *Father, thank You that nothing is impossible with You, in Jesus' name.*
2. *Lord, increase my faith and help me believe beyond what I can see, in Jesus' name.*
3. *You Mountain standing against my family's breakthrough, be moved now, in Jesus' name.*
4. *Father, I receive power to declare and act on Your Word, no matter the circumstance, in Jesus' name.*
5. *O Lord, let my life become proof that faith unlocks supernatural results, in Jesus' name.*
6. *I declare: I walk by faith and not by sight. The impossible in my life will become possible, in Jesus' name.*

Wednesday 5 November **RECOVERING WASTED YEARS**

Read: 1 Kings 18:42-46

Bible in 1 year: Zech. 7-10
Bible in 2 years: Rev. 3-4

"I will restore to you the years that the swarming locust has eaten..." (Joel 2:25a).

One way God restores our wasted years is through divine acceleration. God can empower you to catch up with those who have run ahead of you, and even overtake them.

Are you currently in a situation where you feel like your years have been lost, through sin, delay, affliction, or failure? God is about to do something in your life as you pray this season. Friend, the God you serve is not only a restorer of things, He restores time. He is never late. When He shows up, He makes us the latest. This is your time for the recovery of wasted years, in Jesus' name!

In Joel 2:25, God makes an astonishing promise: *"I WILL RESTORE THE YEARS..."* This is divine acceleration, where what was lost over time is supernaturally recovered in a short period. It's not just about getting things back; It's about catching up to divine timing with speed and favor.

Amos 9:13 gives a vivid picture: *"The plowman will overtake the reaper..."* In other words, harvests will come faster than the sowing. This is not natural; it is supernatural.

When Elijah prayed for rain, it came suddenly, after years of drought (1 Kings 18). And when it did, the hand of the Lord came upon him, and he outran Ahab's chariots. That's divine speed – God making you move faster than you ever could on your own.

Maybe you feel left behind spiritually, financially, relationally, or emotionally. But God can restore wasted years and give you back-to-back breakthroughs. Stay aligned, stay faithful, and get ready. Acceleration is coming!

Let us pray

1. *Father, thank You for being my Restorer of lost years and wasted seasons, in Jesus' name.*
2. *O Lord, heal the wounds of delay, regret, and missed opportunities in my family, in Jesus' name.*
3. *O Father, please, restore everything the enemy, sin, or carelessness has stolen from us, in Jesus' name.*
4. *Father, release divine acceleration over my calling, finances, relationships, and family, in Jesus' name.*
5. *Father, let this be a season of rapid restoration, supernatural progress, and undeniable results, in Jesus' name.*
6. *I declare: The years I lost are being restored. I move forward in divine speed and full recovery, in Jesus' name.*

Thursday 6 November **SUDDEN TURNAROUNDS**

Read: Acts 16:19-34

Bible in 1 year: 1 Tim. 1-3
Bible in 2 years: Rev. 5-6

"Suddenly there was a great earthquake, so that the foundations of the prison were shaken..." (Acts 16:26).

Some breakthroughs unfold gradually, but others happen in an instant. When God steps into a situation, years of bondage can be overturned in a single moment. Paul and Silas experienced such a supernatural turnaround. They were not only imprisoned but locked in the innermost cell, their feet fastened in stocks. By every natural measure, they were trapped. Yet instead of surrendering to despair, they chose to pray and sing hymns to God.

At midnight, the darkest hour, heaven responded. Suddenly, an earthquake shook the prison to its foundations. Every door flew open, and every chain fell off. There were no guards unlocking keys, no legal negotiations, only divine intervention. Scripture reminds us, *"Weeping may endure for a night, but joy comes in the morning" (Psalm 30:5).* The darkest season can become the doorway to your greatest breakthrough.

The word "Suddenly" in Greek is *'Aphno,'* meaning unexpectedly, instantly, without warning. It describes God's power to break into human history with decisive action. One moment of divine interruption can accomplish what human

33

effort could never achieve. *"Is anything too hard for the Lord?" (Genesis 18:14)*. The answer is no! His power knows no limit.

Today, God still specializes in midnight miracles. Your song in the night or prayer in the midst of pain will detonate heaven's intervention. Know this: Your prayer and praise are not weak responses; they are spiritual weapons that shake unseen foundations.

Think of a light switch in a dark room. The darkness may feel overwhelming, but with a single flick, the atmosphere shifts instantly. As you release your faith-filled prayer and praise this week, God's power will bring light and liberty in sudden ways in your life.

Do not underestimate your midnight moments. One "Suddenly" from heaven will cancel your delay and set you on course for destiny.

Let us pray

1. *Father, I thank You for the sudden turnarounds You've prepared for me, in Jesus' name.*
2. *Father, teach me to worship You even in my midnight hour, in Jesus' name.*
3. *Father, let every prison door in my life be shaken and opened by Your power, in Jesus' name.*
4. *Father, arise, let all that has been stagnant in my life be accelerated supernaturally, in Jesus' name.*
5. *Father, visit me in dark moments with divine light and sudden turnaround, in Jesus' name.*
6. *Sudden miracles, breakthroughs, and supernatural results will become common in my life, in Jesus' name.*

Friday 7 November **YOU WILL REAP IN**
DUE SEASON

Read: Ecclesiastes 11:1-6

Bible in 1 year: Ps. 43-45
Bible in 2 years: Rev. 7-8

"Let us not become weary in doing good, for at the proper time we will reap a harvest if we do not give up"
(Galatians 6:9 NIV).

Have you ever been tempted to stop sowing because you feel your labor is fruitless? Listen to this: God has ordained a due season for every seed sown in faith. You will surely reap at the appointed time. Whether it's prayer, service, sacrifice, or obedience, nothing is wasted in the Kingdom. But often, we faint just before the harvest.

Today, Galatians 6:9 reminds you that your harvest is guaranteed, but conditional: *"if we do not give up."* Many individuals and families give up mid-process, often due to fatigue, discouragement from delays, or distractions from trials. But God is not unjust; He will reward every faithful effort (Hebrews 6:10).

Psalm 1 paints the picture of a righteous person like a tree planted by water, yielding fruit in its season. Not before, not after; IN SEASON. Your job is to stay planted, nourished, and consistent. Your harvest will surely come, IN SEASON – at the appointed time.

Ecclesiastes 11 encourages you to sow in the morning and evening, not knowing which seed will produce. The truth is, God causes growth, but you must keep sowing.

Even when nothing seems to change, heaven is tracking every act of faith.

Years ago, I went to meet the man of God, Rev. Ndifor Cletus, with tears in my eyes. I asked a question that had been troubling my heart: "Why am I sowing and not seeing results? I give for God's work faithfully, I give to people, and work hard, but continue to lack." His answer was simple: "Continue to sow, your season of harvest will come. And when it comes, continue to sow to maintain it." It finally came and has never ceased as I keep sowing.

Supernatural results come to those who endure. Don't rush the process or uproot your seed with doubt. Due season always comes if you remain faithful.

Let us pray

1. *Father, thank You because You are faithful to reward every seed sown in obedience; in Jesus' name.*
2. *Father, strengthen me to remain faithful and consistent while waiting for my due season, in Jesus' name.*
3. *I break every spirit of discouragement or delay seeking to abort my harvest, in Jesus' name.*
4. *Father, help me to keep sowing into Your work, my family, destiny, and calling without growing weary, in Jesus' name.*
5. *Father, water my seeds this season and give me supernatural results, in Jesus' name.*
6. *I declare: My due season has come. I will reap a supernatural harvest without delay, in Jesus' name.*

Saturday 8 November   **DON'T QUIT!**

Read: 2 Corinthians 4:13-18

> **Bible in 1 year:** Ps. 46-48
> **Bible in 2 years:** Rev. 9-10

"That is why we never give up. Though our bodies are dying, our spirits are being renewed every day" (2 Corinthians 4:16 NLT).

Life is a battle, so you will always face challenges. At times, pressures mount, strength diminishes, and the temptation to quit becomes high. Yet Paul boldly declares, *"We never give up."* His words carry weight because he had endured much hardship: shipwrecks, imprisonments, betrayals, and bodily weakness. Still, he pressed on, seeing beyond the temporary pain to the eternal glory awaiting him.

Today, Paul reminds us that while our outer man weakens, our inner man is being renewed. The Greek word for renewed is *'anakainoō,'* meaning to be made new, fresh, and renovated in quality. This daily renewal is not human effort but the Spirit of God energizing our souls.

Why should you not quit? First, trials are temporary. Paul calls them "Light afflictions," not because they are easy, but because they are nothing compared to eternal glory. Second, troubles are productive – they produce character, perseverance, and glory. Third, quitting halts this process prematurely. A baobab tree grows from a small seed that has refused to die. Likewise, the believer who persists grows into a mighty testimony and an instrument in God's Kingdom.

Rick Warren once shared how their Church, the Saddleback Church, used seventy-nine different facilities before owning a building. Every Monday, he felt like quitting, yet persistence birthed a global ministry. God is more interested in who you are becoming than in what you are going through.

So, lift your eyes! Fix them not on what is seen but on what is unseen. Your pain has an expiry date, but your glory will last forever, in Jesus' name.

Let us pray

1.	*Father, thank You for my daily renewal and strength through Christ, in Jesus' name.*
2.	*Father, empower me with grace to endure trials and not faint, in Jesus' name.*
3.	*Father, help me to fix my heart on eternal glory above temporary pain, in Jesus' name.*
4.	*Father, silence fear, doubt, and discouragement in my life, in Jesus' name.*
5.	*Father, let my trials produce character and testimonies for Your glory, in Jesus' name.*
6.	*I declare I will not quit – I will finish strong in Christ's glory, in Jesus' name.*

Sunday 9 November   **GRACE THAT MULTIPLIES RESULTS**

Read: Luke 5:1-7

Bible in 1 year: Ps. 49-51

Bible in 2 years: Rev. 11-12

"And God is able to bless you abundantly, so that in all things at all times, having all that you need, you will abound in every good work" (2 Corinthians 9:8 NIV).

There is a dimension of grace that does not merely help you survive but empowers you to overflow. This is supernatural grace, and it produces multiplied results. God's grace multiplies effort, accelerates progress, and amplifies impact. Where others strive and wear out, grace makes the difference.

The Greek word for grace is *'Charis,'* meaning favor, divine influence upon the heart, and its reflection in life. Grace is not passive; it is an active force that transforms ordinary lives into extraordinary vessels. Paul testified, *"I labored more abundantly than they all—yet not I, but the grace of God which was with me" (1 Corinthians 15:10).* With grace, you accomplish what human effort alone could never achieve.

Scripture confirms this in several places: *"But to each one of us grace was given according to the measure of Christ's gift" (Ephesians 4:7), "My grace is sufficient for you, for My strength is made perfect in weakness" (2 Corinthians 12:9),* and *"From His fullness we have all received grace upon grace" (John 1:16).* Grace is abundant, sufficient, and continually supplied for every believer.

A striking example is found in Luke 5:1-7. Peter and his companions fished all night and caught nothing. Exhausted and discouraged, they were ready to quit. But at Jesus' word, they let down their nets again, and caught so many fish that their nets began to break. What long hours of toil could not produce, grace supplied in a moment.

Are you facing limitations today? Ask boldly for grace. One touch of God's empowering presence can turn years of delay into moments of acceleration. Grace doesn't just restore; it multiplies.

Let us pray

1. *Father, I thank You for Your abundant grace at work in my life, in Jesus' name.*
2. *Lord, empower me to do what I could never do in my own strength, in Jesus' name.*
3. *Father, let Your grace cause me to abound in every good work, in Jesus' name.*
4. *Father, I receive grace to labor with ease and wisdom, not in stress and toil, in Jesus' name.*
5. *O Father, let Your grace take me where effort cannot, in Jesus' name.*
6. *I decree that supernatural grace is multiplying results in my life now, in Jesus' name.*

Monday 10 November　　　**BLESSED BEYOND
LIMITS**

Read: Genesis 12:1-3;
　　　　　Numbers 6:22-27

Bible in 1 year: Ps. 52-54
Bible in 2 years: Rev. 13-14

*"Let peoples serve you, and nations bow down to you.
Be master over your brethren, and let your mother's
sons bow down to you. Cursed be everyone who curses
you, and blessed be those who bless you!" (Genesis
27:29).*

Supernatural results begin when we believe God's
spoken Word. In Genesis 27, Isaac unknowingly
released a prophetic blessing over Jacob, words that
shaped Jacob's destiny forever. This wasn't mere
encouragement or a hopeful wish. It was a heaven-
sanctioned declaration that aligned Jacob with supernatural
favor, dominion, and protection.

　　　Once spoken, the blessing could not be reversed.
This is the essence of the prophetic blessing – a verbal
impartation by a spiritual authority that invokes the power
of God into someone's life. John Hagee calls it "A sculptor
of destiny," and the Scriptures affirm it through the lives of
Jacob, Joseph, and even Jesus, who released prophetic
blessings on His disciples (Luke 24:50-51).

　　　"Bless" in Hebrew is *'Barak.'* This root word is
linked with "Kneeling" and "To empower to prosper." It's
not just about speaking well of someone, but also about

41

empowering them with divine enablement. To bless is to empower someone to succeed by heaven's standards.

The prophetic blessing is supernatural because: (1) It can outlast opposition (as seen in Jacob vs. Esau). (2) It cannot be reversed by man. (3) It draws God's favor, even over flawed people (Jacob was imperfect, but still favored). (4) It is multigenerational. Consider the Jewish people – less than 0.2% of the world population, yet they have won over 27% of all Nobel Prizes. This is no accident; it's the enduring power of the prophetic blessing, passed on to them from Abraham and weekly in Jewish homes.

Rev. John Hagee recounts in his church how parents were taught to bless their children. One father spoke over his child, "You are going to be a leader and not a follower. You will rise with excellence." That boy, who struggled with grades and confidence, was transformed; his grades rose, and so did his confidence. That is supernatural transformation through the prophetic blessing.

Let us pray
1. *Father, thank You for the covenant of the blessing passed down through generations to me.*
2. *Father, thank You for the power of Your spoken Word in our lives, in Jesus' name.*
3. *Lord, help me recognize and receive prophetic blessings with faith and reverence, in Jesus' name.*
4. *Father, let every word of curse or limitation spoken over me be reversed by the power of the blessing, in Jesus' name.*
5. *O Lord, I ask for the grace to bless my children, family, and others with intentionality and prophetic insight, in Jesus' name.*

6. *I decree that I am blessed and not cursed, above only and not beneath. My life is marked for supernatural results, in Jesus' name.*

Prophetic Prayers of the Week

1. *"The Lord will fight for you"* (Exod. 14:14); *Every battle in my life will end in supernatural victory, in Jesus' name.*
2. "It shall not come near you" (Ps. 91:7); *Destruction will not touch my family, in Jesus' name.*
3. *"The blessing of Abraham is yours"* (Gal. 3:14); *I walk in covenant blessings, in Jesus' name.*

Tuesday 11 November　　　**LEARN FROM YOUR PAIN**

Read: Psalm 119:65-72

> **Bible in 1 year:** Ps. 55-57
> **Bible in 2 years:** Rev. 15-16

"Before I was afflicted I went astray, but now I obey your word" (Psalm 119:67 NIV).

Pain is one of God's greatest teachers. Job 36:15 says, *"God teaches people through suffering and uses distress to open their eyes."* Though none of us desire hardship, it is often in affliction that we gain the most profound lessons of life.

Every painful experience you go through can become a door of promotion. If you surrender yourself in God's hands, He will use the painful situation to shape your heart, redirect your path, and draw you closer to Himself. The Hebrew word for *"Afflicted"* in Psalm 119:67 is *'anah,'* meaning "To humble, to be bowed down." Affliction bends us low so that our eyes can look upward to God.

David confessed that before affliction, he strayed from God's commandments, but after experiencing pain, he learned to obey God's Word. Pain humbles us, dismantles our pride, and teaches us to trust God wholeheartedly. I know a very troublesome man who became very humble after God saved him from a deadly accident.

Also, through pain, we learn dependence, for weakness reveals God's sustaining power and grace. Furthermore, we learn obedience, for suffering presses us into God's promises and reminds us that His Word is our anchor in the storm. Finally, pain teaches us that we need others. Without trials, some would never admit their need for community, but pain awakens us to the truth that we are not meant to walk alone.

In African villages, a cracked clay pot may appear useless, yet when carried along a path, its cracks drip water that causes flowers to bloom. The very brokenness that seemed shameful becomes the source of life to others. Likewise, our pain, when surrendered to God, can refresh, inspire, and bring healing to those around us.

Friend, are you experiencing affliction? Do not despise it. Let it refine your character, deepen your trust, and serve as a testimony to future generations. Pain may bend you, but it will not break you when God is your teacher.

Let us pray

1. *Father, thank You for the wisdom hidden in painful seasons, in Jesus' name.*
2. *O Father, help me depend on Your strength when I feel weak, in Jesus' name.*
3. *Father, teach me to obey Your Word even through affliction, in Jesus' name.*
4. *Father, turn my present pain into a testimony that blesses others, in Jesus' name.*
5. *Father, surround me with people who will walk with me in trial, in Jesus' name.*
6. *I declare that my pain will produce glory, healing, and impact for generations, in Jesus' name.*

Wednesday 12 November   **THE COST OF WORSHIP**

Read: Numbers 7:1-17

> **Bible in 1 year:** Eze. 1-3
> **Bible in 2 years:** Rev. 17-18

"I will not sacrifice to the Lord my God burnt offerings that cost me nothing" (2 Samuel 24:24).

Genuine worship and kingdom service demand sacrifice; they will always cost you something.

Numbers 7 records the dedication of the tabernacle, where each of the twelve tribal leaders of Israel brought identical offerings to the Lord. Their gifts were costly – silver vessels, golden dishes filled with incense, and twenty-one animals per leader for sacrifice. In today's terms, each leader's offering was worth over thirteen million three hundred and eighty thousand francs ($24,000), with the collective total nearing one hundred and sixty-seven million two hundred and fifty thousand francs ($300,000).

This passage reminds us that worship in God's kingdom has always been costly. True worship is not about convenience, but about devotion and sacrifice. King David understood this principle when he said, *"I will not sacrifice to the Lord my God burnt offerings that cost me nothing" (2 Samuel 24:24).* Worship that costs us nothing is worth nothing.

The leaders in Numbers 7 gave not only valuable items but also their obedience. Every gift was the same, not to compete with one another, but to honor God in unity. This teaches us that worship is not measured by how much we give compared to others, but by the sincerity of our obedience.

Moreover, their offerings involved sacrifice. Animals were central to their livelihood, representing wealth, security, and provision. By offering them to God, they declared that He was their true source. Worship always calls us to release something precious, whether time, pride, possessions, or personal desires, because God is worthy of our best.

Today, the same principle applies. Our worship may not involve silver platters or bulls, but it does involve giving God our wholehearted devotion. When we worship with obedience and sacrifice, God takes notice. Numbers 7 carefully records each offering, showing that He values both the gift and the heart behind it.

Let us pray

1. *Thank You, Lord, for the privilege of offering my life and resources to You.*
2. *Father, teach me to worship You with my best, not my leftovers.*
3. *Father, align my heart with obedience in every act of worship.*
4. *Father, deliver my heart from the attachment to possessions and pride, so I may worship freely, in Jesus' name.*
5. *O Lord Jesus, let my sacrifices to You be expressions of love, not obligation.*
6. *I declare that I will no longer offer meaningless and costless worship to God, in Jesus' name.*

Thursday 13 November   **SUPERNATURAL**
                               SUPPLY IN
                               SCARCITY

Read: 1 Kings 17:13-16

> **Bible in 1 year:** Eze, 4-7
> **Bible in 2 years:** Rev. 19-20

"And my God shall supply all your need according to His riches in glory by Christ Jesus" (Philippians 4:19).

God is Jehovah Jireh, the Lord who provides. He can meet every need you face, in every season and in every situation. In a season of national drought and famine, God sent the prophet Elijah to a widow who had only a handful of flour and a little oil. She was preparing her last meal, expecting death for herself and her son. But God had another plan: supernatural supply in the face of scarcity.

Elijah's instruction may have sounded unreasonable: *"Make me a small cake first" (1Kings 17:13)*. Yet obedience became the key to supernatural provision. The bowl of flour was not used up, and the jar of oil did not run dry. This miracle was not an overflow of abundance but a steady flow of sufficiency. Each day, as she trusted and obeyed, God renewed her supply.

The Greek word for "*Supply*" in Philippians 4:19 is *'Plēroō,'* meaning *to fill, complete, or make full to the brim.* This shows that God's provision is not partial or temporary but complete and ongoing. He doesn't need a warehouse of resources to sustain you; just your faith and obedience.

Think of a cell phone battery connected to a charger. Without the charger, the battery drains. But once connected, power flows continuously, keeping it alive. In the same way, when we stay connected to God through trust and obedience, His unseen supply sustains us even in dry seasons.

Are you facing financial strain, emotional emptiness, or uncertainty about the future? Don't let visible scarcity blind you to God's invisible supply. His Word is your guarantee. What He promises, He sustains.

Remember: **God doesn't bless you based on what you hold in your hand; He blesses you based on what He has spoken over your life.**

Let us pray

1. *Father, I thank You for being my Provider, even in seasons of scarcity, in Jesus' name.*
2. *Father, strengthen my faith to trust You when resources seem limited, in Jesus' name.*
3. *Father, let my "Jar and oil" never run dry according to Your Word, in Jesus' name.*
4. *Father, help me to obey Your instruction, even when it beats my understanding, in Jesus' name.*
5. *O Father, in every area of lack, show Yourself as my supernatural source, in Jesus' name.*
6. *I decree that I am walking in supernatural provision; my supply will not run dry, in Jesus' name.*

Friday 14 November　　　　**BREAK THE**
　　　　　　　　　　　　　　　　　ENEMY'S CONTROL

Read: Acts 13:6-12

> **Bible in 1 year:** Eze. 8-11
> **Bible in 2 years:** Rev. 21-22

"Every place that the sole of your foot will tread upon I have given to you, just as I promised to Moses" (Joshua 1:3).

Unseen spiritual forces often control territories. That is why you may experience spiritual battles and confrontations when you move into a new territory.

Satan works through agents, both conscious and unconscious, to hinder the spread of God's kingdom. In Acts 13, Elymas the sorcerer opposed Paul and Barnabas, attempting to prevent the proconsul from receiving the gospel. But Paul, filled with the Holy Spirit, confronted him directly and broke his influence with words of divine authority. The result was immediate: the sorcerer's control was shattered, and the proconsul believed in Christ.

This passage reminds us that the gospel is not only about preaching but also about confronting and disarming the powers of darkness over territories. Jesus Himself declared, *"All authority in heaven and on earth has been given to me. Therefore, go and make disciples…" (Matthew 28:18-19).* Believers are sent into territories with the authority of Christ to confront spiritual resistance and impose order.

Throughout Scripture, God's servants confronted territorial powers. Moses challenged Pharaoh, whose

50

magicians tried to replicate God's wonders but were ultimately defeated (Exodus 7:11-12). Elijah confronted the prophets of Baal on Mount Carmel, and fire from heaven silenced idolatry (1 Kings 18:36-39). In the New Testament, Jesus cast out legions of demons from a man in the Gerasenes, setting him free and transforming the region (Mark 5:1-20).

Beloved, every territory, be it your family, workplace, or community, faces the influence of agents of darkness. Some distract, others manipulate, while some spread fear and lies. But you are not powerless. The same Spirit who filled Paul is in you. Stand firm, discern the enemy's tactics, and use the authority of Christ through prayer, fasting, and the Word. Darkness cannot rule where the light of Christ is released.

Let us pray

1. *Father, I thank You for giving me authority in Christ over all powers of darkness, in Jesus' name.*
2. *Lord, open my eyes to discern the activities of demonic agents in my territory, in Jesus' name.*
3. *By the authority of Christ, I break the influence of sorcery, witchcraft, and manipulation in my environment, in Jesus' name.*
4. *Father, empower me by the Holy Spirit to stand boldly like Paul and confront evil without fear, in Jesus' name.*
5. *Lord, let the Gospel spread in my territory with power, and let every veil of darkness be torn away, in Jesus' name.*
6. *I declare that no agent of darkness shall control my family, community, or destiny; Christ rules in my territory, in Jesus' name.*

Saturday 15 November

DOMINION OVER GENERATIONAL CURSES

Read: Galatians 3:13-14;
Colossians 2:14-15

Bible in 1 year: Eze. 12-14
Bible in 2 years: Hos. 1-2

"Christ has redeemed us from the curse of the law, having become a curse for us..." (Galatians 3:13).

Are you experiencing repeated cycles of failure, premature death, and unexplainable oppression? These are often the signs of generational curses – evil covenants or demonic altars established by ancestors. But the Good news is: Jesus came to break every curse and transfer us into the lineage of blessing and dominion.

Galatians 3:13 says Christ became a curse for us. He absorbed every legal claim of Satan against your family line. Colossians 2:14-15 adds that Jesus *"wiped out the handwriting of requirements"* and disarmed the enemy at the cross. Satan has no legal ground to torment you with a generational curse. As a believer in Christ, you are no longer supposed to suffer the consequences of your parents' sin.

The Hebrew word for "Curse" is *'arar*, meaning "To bind with a spell, hem in with obstacles." Christ reversed that sentence by His blood. In Him, you are no longer bound, you are blessed like Abraham. You are not trapped; you are free! Claim it authoritatively.

Numbers 23:23 declares, *"There is no enchantment against Jacob."* You now belong to the spiritual lineage of

Abraham through faith. The old order is broken. No curse can cancel the blessing you have received in Christ.

You must rise and enforce your new identity. Stop agreeing with ancestral labels. Speak with kingdom boldness. Cancel every legal ground the enemy holds against you. Through prayer, confession, and alignment with God's Word, walk out of bondage and into the blessing.

Jesus didn't just save your soul; He rewrote your spiritual DNA. Your bloodline is royal. You carry the Lion's name. You are no longer a victim of ancestral altars; you are a living altar for God's glory.

Let us pray

1. *Father, thank You for redeeming me from every generational curse through the blood of Jesus, in Jesus' name.*
2. *I renounce every known and unknown ancestral covenant operating in my family, in Jesus' name.*
3. *Arise, Father, let every evil altar and pattern working against my destiny be destroyed by fire, in Jesus' name.*
4. *I declare that I have a new spiritual DNA in Christ; I am free from every family bondage, in Jesus' name.*
5. *Dear Holy Spirit, establish a new generational blessing in my family line, in Jesus' name.*
6. *I declare: I am redeemed by the blood, crowned with favor, and walking in generational dominion, in Jesus' name.*

Sunday 16 November　　　**PROPHETIC INSIGHT AND GUIDANCE**

Read: 2 Kings 6:8-17

> **Bible in 1 year:** Eze. 15-18
> **Bible in 2 years:** Hos. 3-4

"When the Spirit of truth comes, He will guide you into all truth..." (John 16:13a NLT).

I n uncertain times, what you need most is not just common sense; it is prophetic insight and supernatural guidance. God desires to lead you by the Holy Spirit into accurate understanding, divine timing, and strategic decisions.

In 2 Kings 6, Elisha demonstrated prophetic sensitivity by revealing the enemy's secret military plans to Israel, again and again. What could have ended in the defeat of Israel turned into victory through supernatural guidance.

The Hebrew word for "I*nsight*" often relates to *'Binah,'* meaning "Understanding, discernment, or perception." Insight is more than knowledge; it is the ability to see beneath the surface, to grasp God's perspective on a given situation.

Can we operate with such insight? Yes! Jesus promised that the Holy Spirit would guide us into all truth (John 16:13). That includes clarity in confusion, protection from traps, and wisdom for crucial decisions. The sons of Issachar were praised because they *"Understood the times and knew what Israel should do" (1 Chronicles 12:32)*. This kind of prophetic discernment is vital for your family, leadership, and the pursuit of your destiny.

I want you to know that prophetic insight is not reserved for prophets alone; in the New Testament, it is the inheritance of every believer who walks with the Spirit. You cultivate it through prayer, meditating on the Word, and remaining sensitive to God's whisper.

Think of a traveler with a GPS. Without direction, he may wander aimlessly, wasting time and energy. But with guidance, he arrives quickly and safely. In the same way, one word from God can save you from years of error and position you for supernatural advancement.

As A.W. Tozer once said, *"The man who walks with God will always reach his destination."* Friend, stop guessing. Stop reacting. Ask the Lord to open your eyes. When you see through God's eyes, you walk in supernatural results.

Let us pray

1. *Father, thank You for giving me the Holy Spirit to guide me into all truth, in Jesus' name.*
2. *O Lord, open my spiritual eyes and sharpen my prophetic discernment, in Jesus' name.*
3. *Father, expose every trap of the enemy and lead me in paths of victory this season, in Jesus' name.*
4. *Father, let my family walk in divine direction and accurate decisions this season, in Jesus' name.*
5. *Father, cause me to discern times, seasons, and divine instructions with precision, in Jesus' name.*
6. *I declare: I walk in prophetic insight and supernatural guidance, and will not miss my appointments this season, in Jesus' name.*

STOP THAT SUDDEN ATTACK

Read: Mark 4:35-41

> **Bible in 1 year:** Eze. 19-21
> **Bible in 2 years:** Hos. 5-6

"He got up, rebuked the wind and said to the waves, 'Quiet! Be still!' Then the wind died down and it was completely calm" (Mark 4:39).

L ife often brings sudden attacks that catch us unprepared. These are ambushes of the enemy designed to shake our faith, disrupt our peace, and stop our progress.

In Mark 4, Jesus and His disciples were crossing to the other side with a divine mission ahead, to set a man free from demonic bondage in the region of the Gadarenes. Suddenly, a violent storm arose. This was no ordinary weather change but a demonic ambush meant to stop Jesus' assignment, or kill Him.

The disciples panicked, but Jesus, resting in the storm, revealed that true authority over attacks is rooted in confidence in the Father. While the disciples trembled with fear, Jesus stood, rebuked the wind, and commanded the waves to be still. Immediately, peace replaced chaos. This moment teaches us that the enemy's ambush may be sudden, but Christ's authority is greater and final.

"Rebuke" is Greek *'Epitimaō,'* meaning "To command, admonish, or warn sternly." It conveys authority in speech that silences opposition. After Jesus had rebuked and calmed the storm, He turned to the Disciples and rebuked them: "Why are you so afraid? Have you still no faith?" (vs. 40). He expected them to confront the situation rather than cry and complain. You must learn to firmly rebuke the forces of darkness when they rise against you.

Beloved, Satan often attacks when you are closest to a breakthrough, when you are tired, distracted, or celebrating a victory. His goal is to sink your "Boat" before you reach destiny's shore. But you have the same authority Jesus exercised. Through His Spirit, you can rebuke storms of fear, sickness, lack, and opposition. Do not beg the storm to stop. Rebuke it with authority, for in Christ, every storm must bow before you.

Let us pray

1. *Father, thank You for giving me authority in Christ over every storm of life, in Jesus' name.*
2. *Lord, open my eyes to recognize sudden attacks of the enemy before they escalate, in Jesus' name.*
3. *By the authority of Christ, I rebuke every storm of sickness, fear, and confusion around my life, in Jesus' name.*
4. *Lord, strengthen my faith to stand firm in the middle of storms, in Jesus' name.*
5. *Father, release Your peace to rule over every area of my life where the enemy is stirring chaos, in Jesus' name.*
6. *I declare that every sudden attack against my destiny is silenced now by the authority of Jesus Christ, in Jesus' name.*

Prophetic Prayers of the Week

1. *"The Lord is near to all who call on Him"* (Ps. 145:18); *I enjoy divine presence everywhere I go this month, in Jesus' name.*

2. *"Be still and know that I am God"* (Ps. 46:10); *Anxiety shall not rule my heart, in Jesus' name.*
3. *"The righteous flourish like a palm tree"* (Ps. 92:12); *I will flourish spiritually, emotionally, financially, etc., in Jesus' name.*

Tuesday 18 November **NO COVENANT WITH THE WICKED**

Read: 1 Kings 11:1-13

Bible in 1 year: 1 Chron. 1-3
Bible in 2 years: Hos. 7-8

"Do not be unequally yoked together with unbelievers" (2 Corinthians 6:14).

Covenants with the wicked are a satanic strategy to trap and destroy the righteous. Watch out! Solomon was a man of extraordinary wisdom, yet wisdom without obedience to God is incomplete. In 1 Kings 3:1, he allied with Pharaoh, king of Egypt, by marrying his daughter. What seemed like a wise political strategy eventually became the seed of compromise. This covenant opened the door to idolatry, as Solomon later built shrines for his foreign wives and their gods (1 Kings 11:4-6). God judged him.

The Bible consistently warns against forming covenants with the wicked. Israel was commanded not to make treaties with the nations around them because such alliances would turn their hearts away from the Lord (Deuteronomy 7:2-4). Paul echoes this principle in the New Testament: *"Do not be unequally yoked together with unbelievers" (2 Corinthians 6:14).* Relationships, whether in marriage, business, or friendship, can influence our faith either toward God or toward compromise. I wonder how some people think they can be part of secret societies and still be Christians.

Biblical history shows the horrific consequences of unholy covenants. King Jehoshaphat allied himself with

59

King Ahab, one of Israel's most wicked rulers, and suffered defeat as a result (2 Chronicles 18:28-34). Many Christians backslid because they established unholy covenants with unbelievers.

Beloved, God has called you to holiness and separation. This does not mean isolation from the world, but it does mean you must guard your heart and commitments. Every alliance carries spiritual weight. Ask yourself: Does this relationship strengthen my walk with God or weaken it? May we choose to covenant with Christ above all, for in Him we have eternal life and victory.

Let us pray

1. *Father, I thank You for bringing me into a covenant of grace through the blood of Jesus, in Jesus' name.*
2. *Lord, give me discernment to avoid ungodly alliances and covenants that can compromise my faith, in Jesus' name.*
3. *Father, deliver me from every wrong commitment or relationship that weakens my walk with You, in Jesus' name.*
4. *Lord, help me to honor my covenant with You through obedience and faithfulness, in Jesus' name.*
5. *Father, surround me with godly relationships that strengthen my destiny and glorify Your name, in Jesus' name.*
6. *I declare that I will not covenant with the wicked; my only lasting covenant is with the Lord Jesus Christ, in Jesus' name.*

Wednesday 19 November   **WAKE UP MOTHERS**

Read: 1 Kings 3:16-28

> **Bible in 1 year:** 1 Chron. 4-6
> **Bible in 2 years:** Hos. 9-10

"She watches over the affairs of her household and does not eat the bread of idleness. Her children arise and call her blessed; her husband also, and he praises her" (Proverbs 31:27-28).

Motherhood is more than giving birth; it is a sacred responsibility to nurture, protect, and preserve destinies. Many mothers still do not understand that it is a tough battle to raise godly children in this generation. If you don't wake up, the enemy may frustrate the destinies of your children.

In 1 Kings 3, two women stood before Solomon, both claiming the same child. The true mother proved herself not by argument but by her willingness to sacrifice for the life of her child. She stayed alert to her child's needs and refused to let death or deception rob her of her son.

When mothers "Sleep," children suffer. To sleep here means to become absent, passive, or disengaged. Many destinies have been derailed because mothers failed to watch. In Scripture, Jochebed, the mother of Moses, stayed spiritually awake. While other babies were thrown into the Nile, she hid her son and later placed him in a basket of faith (Exodus 2:1-4). Her vigilance preserved Israel's future deliverer. Hannah, too, stayed awake in prayer until God gave her Samuel, whom she dedicated to the Lord (1 Samuel 1:10-11, 27-28).

Mothers and fathers alike must understand: to neglect children is to expose them to premature destruction. Beloved, children today are under fierce attack – from wrong ideologies, peer pressure, addictions, and forces of darkness. Mothers (and parents in general) must rise in prayer, mentorship, and active involvement.

To stay awake is to intercede for your children daily, to meet their needs, to protect them, to correct them, and to guard their destinies. Your watchfulness can determine the future of your children.

Let us pray

1. *Father, I thank You for the gift of children and the responsibility to watch over them, in Jesus' name.*
2. *Lord, forgive me for every area where I have been passive or distracted concerning my children's destiny, in Jesus' name.*
3. *Father, give me the grace to stay spiritually alert and to intercede constantly for my children, in Jesus' name.*
4. *Lord, protect children everywhere from premature death, deception, and destruction, in Jesus' name.*
5. *Father, raise mothers and fathers in this generation who will guard the next generation with wisdom and prayer, in Jesus' name.*
6. *I declare that my children's destinies will not be stolen or destroyed; they shall live to fulfill God's purpose, in Jesus' name.*

Thursday 20 November **PRAY THIS BEFORE YOU SLEEP**

Read: John 14:15- 26

Bible in 1 year: 1 Chron. 7-9
Bible in 2 years: Hos. 11-12

"But the Helper, the Holy Spirit, whom the Father will send in my name, he will teach you all things and bring to your remembrance all that I have said to you" (John 14:26).

God has designed sleep to be a time of renewal, both physically and spiritually. Sleep is not simply the end of the day; it is a moment to draw near to God and entrust ourselves into His care. Before you close your eyes, commune with the Holy Spirit, for He desires to fill, teach, protect, and renew you.

1. *Holy Spirit, Fill Me:* Each day drains our strength and focus. But when the Spirit fills us, He restores our hearts and minds with God's presence. Ephesians 5:18 reminds us, *"Be filled with the Spirit."* As He fills you, anxiety is replaced with peace and emptiness with joy.

2. *Holy Spirit, Teach Me:* The Spirit is the best teacher. He guides us into truth, even in our sleep. Job 33:15-16 says God instructs men through dreams and visions of the night. Invite Him to deposit wisdom, ideas, and spiritual insight into your heart as you rest.

63

3. **Holy Spirit, Protect Me:** Night is often a time of vulnerability. David prayed, *"In peace I will lie down and sleep, for you alone, Lord, make me dwell in safety" (Psalm 4:8).* Ask the Spirit to surround you like a shield, guarding you against fear, nightmares, and demonic attacks.

4. **Holy Spirit, Renew Me:** Sleep is God's design for restoration. Isaiah 40:31 says those who wait on the Lord will renew their strength. As you sleep, the Spirit refreshes your body and revives your spirit for a new day of service.

Beloved, bedtime is not just a routine; it is an invitation. End your day with the Holy Spirit, and you will wake up strengthened, guided, and covered by His presence.

Let us pray
1. *Father, I thank You for the gift of the Holy Spirit, my Comforter and Guide, in Jesus' name.*
2. *Holy Spirit, fill me afresh tonight with Your presence and peace, in Jesus' name.*
3. *Holy Spirit, teach me divine wisdom and reveal to me the Father's heart even as I rest, in Jesus' name.*
4. *Lord, protect me and my household through the night from all fear, danger, and attacks, in Jesus' name.*
5. *Holy Spirit, renew my body, soul, and spirit as I sleep, and prepare me for tomorrow, in Jesus' name.*
6. *I declare that I will rest in safety, covered and strengthened by the Holy Spirit, in Jesus' name.*

Friday 21 November　　　　**THE GOD OF**
　　　　　　　　　　　　　　SUDDEN
　　　　　　　　　　　　　　INTERVENTION

Read: Judges 15:9-17

Bible in 1 year: 1 Chron. 10-13
Bible in 2 years: Hos. 13-14

"The Lord, whom you seek, will suddenly come to His temple" (Malachi 3:1).

God specializes in stepping into impossible situations at the very moment when human strength and resources have failed. He will intervene for you this month, in Jesus' mighty name!

Samson, bound with new ropes and handed over to the Philistines, looked like a man defeated. His enemies shouted in triumph; certain the story was over. Yet Scripture declares that suddenly the Spirit of the Lord came upon him, and the ropes fell as if they were nothing. He slaughtered a thousand of them with a common jawbone. In an instant, what seemed like bondage turned into deliverance and victory.

This is the pattern of God's intervention. He often waits until the enemy has celebrated, so that His glory alone is revealed. When Israel was trapped between Pharaoh's army and the Red Sea, it seemed like total annihilation. Yet suddenly the Lord opened a path through the waters (Exodus 14:21-22). When Shadrach, Meshach, and Abednego were thrown into the blazing furnace, everyone expected them to be reduced to ashes. But suddenly the king saw a fourth Man in the fire, and the flames could not harm them (Daniel 3:24-25). When Peter was imprisoned, chained between soldiers, the church prayed. That very night, suddenly an angel appeared, and the chains fell off (Acts 12:6-7).

Suddenly is Hebrew *'Pithom,'* meaning unexpectedly, without warning, describing a divine interruption that instantly changes the course of events.

Beloved, the enemy may think he has you cornered, but God is the master of sudden reversals. His intervention comes without warning, but always on time. The same Spirit who empowered Samson is at work in you through Christ Jesus. Hold on, trust Him, and do not let fear dictate your response. For when God steps in, every chain must break, every prison door must open, and every enemy must bow, in Jesus' name.

Let us pray

1. *Father, I thank You for being the God who intervenes suddenly in the lives of Your children, in Jesus' name.*
2. *O Lord, arise suddenly in every situation where I am trapped, and show forth Your power, in Jesus' name.*
3. *I receive the fire of the Holy Spirit like Samson, to break every chain of limitation, in Jesus' name.*
4. *Father, let sudden deliverance come into my family, ministry, and destiny today, in Jesus' name.*
5. *Lord, let sudden breakthroughs and sudden victories silence the triumph of the enemy in my life and family, in Jesus' name.*
6. *I declare that sudden divine intervention is my portion; my enemies will not rejoice over me, in Jesus' name.*

Saturday 22 November   **HOW TO DEFEAT THE DEVIL**

Read: Colossians 2:13-15

Bible in 1 year: 1 Chron. 14-16
Bible in 2 years: Joel 1-2

"And they overcame him by the blood of the Lamb and by the word of their testimony, and they did not love their lives to the death" (Revelation 12:11).

The Bible makes it clear: you cannot kill the devil, imprison him, or stop him from ever attacking you or your family. His presence, attacks, and schemes are real. However, though he is persistent, he is already a defeated foe. The victory of Jesus Christ at the cross sealed his defeat forever.

Colossians 2:15 declares that Jesus disarmed principalities and powers, triumphing over them publicly. Our task is not to destroy the devil but to enforce Christ's victory over him.

How then do you defeat him in your daily life?

First, by knowing your identity in Christ. Satan thrives on lies and deception, but when you stand firm in the truth of who you are – a redeemed child of God, seated with Christ in heavenly places, you can resist his influence (Ephesians 2:6). Jesus defeated Satan in the wilderness not with human strength but by declaring, *"It is written"* (Matthew 4:4, 7, 10). Authority flows from the Word.

Second, you overcome the devil through the blood of Jesus. The blood cleanses you, protects you, and gives you access to God's throne of grace (Hebrews 10:19). Satan cannot stand against you if you know the power of the blood.

Third, you defeat him through the word of your testimony. Publicly declare what Christ has done and confess His promises over your life. Silence often gives Satan room, but bold confession brings victory.

Biblical examples confirm this. Jesus Himself triumphed over Satan in the wilderness with the Word. Paul cast out the spirit of divination from a slave girl in Philippi, silencing demonic manipulation (Acts 16:16-18). The early church stood boldly against persecution, refusing to compromise even when threatened with death. They overcame not by fear but by faith in Christ.

Beloved, you cannot negotiate with the devil. But in Christ, you are more than a conqueror.

Let us pray

1. *Father, thank You for the victory Christ has already won over Satan, in Jesus' name.*
2. *Lord, open my eyes to fully understand my identity and authority in Christ, in Jesus' name.*
3. *By the blood of Jesus, I silence every accusation of the enemy against my life, in Jesus' name.*
4. *Lord, strengthen me to stand firm in the Word, resisting every temptation of Satan, in Jesus' name.*
5. *Father, let my testimony of Christ's goodness destroy every lie of the enemy in my territory, in Jesus' name.*
6. *I declare that I am an overcomer; the devil is defeated and Christ reigns in my life, in Jesus' name.*

Sunday 23 November **GOD'S TIMING AND GENERATIONAL FRUITFULNESS**

Read: Genesis 21:1-7;
Psalm 105:17-24

Bible in 1 year: 1 Chron. 17-19
Bible in 2 years: Joel 3; Amos 1

"He has made everything beautiful in its time"
(Ecclesiastes 3:11a NIV).

Do you feel like you are late in life? Is there a voice telling you that God has forgotten you? Things are about to change. Friend, God works in seasons, not seconds. What may feel like a delay is often divine alignment.

Abraham and Sarah waited decades for Isaac. But when God's time came, the barrenness ended, and laughter filled their home (Genesis 21:6). You too will soon laugh, in Jesus' name!

Behind the scenes, God was not only preparing a child; He was establishing a generational lineage that would multiply across nations.

Joseph's story is another example. Betrayed, imprisoned, and forgotten, it seemed his dreams had died. But in God's perfect time, he was elevated, and his family was preserved through him (Psalm 105:17–22). Israel later multiplied in Egypt, fulfilling the original promise God made to Abraham (Exodus 1:7).

God's timing produces fruit that outlives us. What He begins in one generation often matures in another. If you give up in your waiting season, you may forfeit blessings meant for your children and grandchildren. Impatience leads to short-term decisions. But those who trust God's time walk into long-term, generational fruitfulness. You're not just waiting for personal results; you are sowing for a family legacy.

No matter how barren your current season feels, keep sowing. Stay faithful. God's clock is never late. He will make it beautiful in its time.

Let us pray

1. *Father, thank You for making everything beautiful in its time, including my family's destiny, in Jesus' name.*

2. *Father, help me to trust Your timing, even when I do not understand the delay, in Jesus' name.*

3. *I break the power of the spirit of frustration, haste, and discouragement over my family, in Jesus' name.*

4. *O Father, please, release generational fruitfulness that multiplies beyond my lifetime, in Jesus' name.*

5. *Father, let my obedience today prepare a foundation for blessings in future generations, in Jesus' name.*

6. *Today, I declare: My family will flourish in God's appointed time, and our fruitfulness will outlive us, in Jesus' name.*

Monday 24 November　　　　**BLESSED BY DIVINE**
　　　　　　　　　　　　　　CONNECTIONS

Read: Ruth 2:1-12;
　　　　1 Samuel 18:1-4

Bible in 1 year: 1 Chron. 20:23
Bible in 2 years: Amos 2-3

"Two are better than one, because they have a good return for their labor" (Ecclesiastes 4:9 NIV).

God often releases supernatural results through relationships. A divine connection is a person strategically positioned by God to unlock doors, speak a timely word, offer support, or carry you into your next season.

　　Ruth's life was transformed the day she met Boaz. She did not just meet a kind landowner; she connected with her destiny. That meeting preserved her future, provided for her needs, and positioned her in the very lineage of Christ (Ruth 2). It was not a coincidence but divine orchestration.

　　David's bond with Jonathan became a covenant of protection, encouragement, and loyalty that preserved David's life (1 Samuel 18). Likewise, when Paul faced rejection from the apostles, Barnabas stood by him, defending his testimony and opening the door for his ministry (Acts 9:26-28). One God-ordained relationship can achieve in a moment what human effort struggles to accomplish in years.

　　To picture this, think of a bridge across a raging river. Alone, you cannot cross. But when someone lays the right planks, suddenly the impossible becomes possible.

71

Divine connections act as bridges that carry you safely into your God-prepared destiny.

However, not every relationship is divine. Some connections drain your strength, blur your vision, or derail your assignment. That is why discernment is critical. This end of year, pray not merely for relationships, but for the right relationships – those sent to add, not subtract; to multiply, not divide.

Divine connections will: (1) Announce your name in the right places. (2) Defend your assignment when challenged. (3) Unlock for you hidden favor before kings. (4) Accelerate your journey toward destiny. (5) Sharpen your vision and strengthen your hands in battle.

As John Maxwell said, "One is too small a number to achieve greatness." Supernatural results flow from the blessing of divine connections.

Let us pray

1. *Father, thank You for the people You have assigned to help me fulfill my purpose, in Jesus' name.*
2. *Lord, connect me with the right people and disconnect me from wrong ones, in Jesus' name.*
3. *Father, reveal and release destiny helpers into every area of my life this end of the year, in Jesus' name.*
4. *Father, let divine favor speak through the voices You have assigned to support my journey, in Jesus' name.*
5. *I break loose from every delay caused by wrong associations and I connect to my destiny, in Jesus' name.*
6. *I declare: I walk in the blessing of divine connections. My destiny is accelerated through kingdom relationships, in Jesus' name.*

Prophetic Prayers of the Week

1. *"You anoint my head with oil, my cup runs over"* (Ps. 23:5); *My head will not lack oil this season, in Jesus' name.*

2. *"You will be blessed in the city and in the field"* (Deut. 28:3); *I will prosper everywhere I go, in Jesus' name.*

3. *"The earth is the Lord's and its fullness"* (Ps. 24:1); *I partake of divine abundance, in Jesus' name.*

Tuesday 25 November   **LEAN ON GOD'S PROMISES**

Read: Acts 27:13-44

> **Bible in 1 year:** 1 Chron. 24-26
> **Bible in 2 years:** Amos 4-5

"Not a single one of all the good promises the Lord had given to the family of Israel was left unfulfilled; everything he had spoken came true" (Joshua 21:45, NLT).

The storms of life often expose what we truly trust in – God, man, ourselves, or material things. When problems arise, many people rely on their bank accounts, relationships, or personal abilities, only to discover how quickly these things fail. But God's Word assures us that His promises never fail. Hallelujah! Joshua testified that *"Not a single one of all the good promises the Lord had given…was left unfulfilled."* This truth sustains us when everything else crumbles.

In Acts 27, Paul and his companions faced a fierce storm. The ship was battered, the crew lost hope, and survival seemed impossible. Yet Paul declared, *"So take courage, men, because I believe God that it will be just the way it was told to me."* He did not lean on himself, the captain, the sailors, or the ship itself. He leaned entirely on God's promise, and God kept His Word. The ship broke apart, but every person was saved, just as God had said.

The Greek word for "Promise" is *'epangelia,'* meaning "An announcement of what has been assured." God's promises are not vague wishes but guaranteed declarations backed by His unchanging character. Unlike money, beauty, charm, or human influence, all of which can sink, God's promises endure forever.

An African proverb says, "However long the night, the dawn will break." In the same way, however fierce your storm, God's Word will prevail. You, too, will prevail if you hang onto God's promises. When everything else perishes, His promises remain unshaken. If you lean on them, not only will you find safety, but others connected to you will also be saved, just as Paul's shipmates were.

Trusting God's promises guarantees an incredible turnaround, because everything He has spoken will surely come to pass.

Let us pray

1. *Father, thank You that every promise You have spoken is true and unshakable, in Jesus' name.*
2. *Lord, help me to lean on Your Word when storms threaten my peace, in Jesus' name.*
3. *Father, deliver me from trusting in failing lifeboats of money, beauty, or ability, in Jesus' name.*
4. *Lord, strengthen my faith to believe that Your Word will be fulfilled in my life, in Jesus' name.*
5. *Are you facing a storm right now? Pray Isaiah 41:8-14, 43:1-2; Philippians 1:6.*
6. *I declare that every promise of God over my life shall come to pass with power and glory, in Jesus' name.*

Wednesday 26 November   **LIVING AS A CONSECRATED SACRIFICE**

Read: Numbers 8:5-16

Bible in 1 year: 1 Chron. 27-29
Bible in 2 years: Amos 6-7

"Therefore, I urge you, brothers and sisters, in view of God's mercy, to offer your bodies as a living sacrifice, holy and pleasing to God – this is your true and proper worship" (Romans 12:1).

God expects His children to live in a way that reflects Him. Genuine Christianity begins with the way we live, not with what we have or do for God.

In Numbers 8:5-16, God instructed Moses to consecrate the Levites, setting them apart for holy service in the tabernacle. They were cleansed, washed, and offered before the Lord as living sacrifices, taking the place of Israel's firstborn. Their consecration was more than a ritual. It symbolized total surrender to God's service.

Paul takes this principle further in Romans 12:1. He reminds believers that through Christ, every one of us, in appreciation to the mercies of God manifested towards us, is called to live as a "Living sacrifice," holy and pleasing to God. Unlike the Levites, we are not set apart through ritual washing but through the sacrifice of Jesus and the cleansing of the Holy Spirit. Our lives – our bodies, minds, and actions must become the instruments God uses to accomplish His will on earth.

The word "Sacrifice" in Romans is *'thusia'* in Greek, meaning an offering given wholly to God. Just as the Levites were dedicated to serving, we too are invited to consecrate ourselves daily. This is an act of worship that goes beyond church attendance or religious duty. It is a lifestyle of surrender, obedience, and holiness.

In practical terms, living as a sacrifice means letting God guide your words, decisions, and relationships. Sister Anna, a young professional, saw her workplace as her mission field. She prayed for colleagues, encouraged them, and chose to practice integrity even at a cost. Soon, her office became a place of blessing. Her colleagues began to open up to the Gospel. God was using her daily sacrifices to impact lives.

Friend, the best way to respond to God's mercy is by giving your best to Him in everything, whether at work, at home, or in ministry. It is choosing God's will over your comfort.

Let us pray

1. *Father, thank You for making me holy through Christ, and calling me to serve You.*
2. *Father, help me present my life as a living sacrifice, daily yielding to Your will, in Jesus' name.*
3. *Father, cleanse my heart, mind, and actions; let me be holy as You are holy, in Jesus' name.*
4. *Lord, empower me to serve others with love, reflecting Your presence in my life, in Jesus' name.*
5. *Father, lead every step I take, that it may honor You, in Jesus' name.*
6. *My life is wholly consecrated to God's glory; I walk in holiness, power, and favor, in Jesus' name.*

Thursday 27 November   **IRREVERSIBLE FAVOR**

Read: Numbers 23:19-20

> **Bible in 1 year:** Gen. 27-29
> **Bible in 2 years:** Amos 8-9

"Behold, I have received a command to bless; He has blessed, and I cannot reverse it" (Numbers 23:20).

Divine blessings are irreversible! When Isaac realized he had blessed Jacob instead of Esau, his body trembled. Not out of fear – but because he knew what had just occurred was irrevocable. He said, *"Indeed, he shall be blessed!" (Genesis 27:33).*

This is the nature of the prophetic blessing: once spoken under divine inspiration and authority, it cannot be undone – not by man, not by manipulation, not even by regret. God's Word confirms this in Romans 11:29: *"The gifts and the calling of God are irrevocable."* If He has declared you blessed, there is no power in hell or on earth that can annul that declaration.

This gives believers supreme confidence, not in ourselves, but in God's unchangeable character. As Balaam found out in Numbers 23, *"God is not a man, that He should lie."* When He blesses, it is final. You can't curse what God has already covered. You can't limit what He has already launched. John Hagee puts it like this: "When God Almighty, King of the universe, places His blessing upon you, no person on earth can take it from you, and no power in the universe can eliminate it from your life."

The Hebrew word for *"Bless"* in Numbers 23:20 is *'Barak,'* and the word for *"Reverse"* is *'Shub,'* meaning *to turn back or undo.* Balaam says it plainly: *"God has blessed, and I cannot 'shub' it."* It's locked in. Set in stone – irreversible favor. Even if your journey has detoured, your blessing hasn't. Even if people around you try to sabotage it (like Esau, Haman, or Saul), the oil of God's favor remains. The supernatural results that come with His blessing are not performance-based; they are covenant-based.

No one can un-bless what God has already blessed!

Let us pray

1. *Father, thank You that Your blessings over my life are irrevocable, in Jesus' name.*
2. *Lord, help me rest in Your promises despite circumstances, in Jesus' name.*
3. *Father, please cancel every curse or opposition spoken against my blessing, in Jesus' name.*
4. *O Lord, empower me to walk boldly in what You have declared, in Jesus' name.*
5. *Father, let the fruit of Your blessing manifest in every area of my life and family, in Jesus' name.*
6. *I decree that I am irrevocably blessed; what God has spoken shall stand in my life and family, in Jesus' name.*

Friday 28 November

COURAGE TO DO HIS WILL

Read: Acts 20:22-24

> **Bible in 1 year:** Ps.120-126
>
> **Bible in 2 years:** Obed; Jonah 1

"The wicked flee when no one pursues, but the righteous are bold as a lion" (Proverbs 28:1).

Sometimes, doing God's will is like walking into the mouth of a lion – terrifying, yet necessary. It demands a kind of courage not born of human willpower, but of the Holy Spirit.

This is the courage Paul exemplified in Acts 20. Though prophets warned him of suffering in Jerusalem, he declared, *"I am going to Jerusalem, constrained by the Spirit" (vs. 22).* His obedience stemmed from deep intimacy with God, where pleasing the Spirit mattered more than preserving his own life.

Some claim Paul was misguided for ministering among the Jews, insisting that his calling was solely to the Gentiles. Yet persecution followed him in both arenas, not because of where he went, but because of what he preached. The gospel, by nature, confronts darkness and provokes resistance.

Despite his arrest in Jerusalem, imprisonment, beatings, and betrayal, Paul's obedience bore lasting fruit. From his prison cell, he penned four epistles: Ephesians, Philippians, Colossians, and Philemon, and led members of Caesar's household to Christ. Even in chains, the Word of God was not bound.

However, courageous obedience faces three major tests: the fear of standing alone, the fear of suffering, and the fear of death. These fears are powerful, but not insurmountable. The Greek word for courage, *'Tharseo,'* means to take heart, not because of confidence in self, but confidence in God's plan. True courage is moving forward despite fear, trusting that obedience will always bring glory to God.

Are you at a crossroads, knowing God's will yet frozen by fear? Ask the Holy Spirit to fill you with divine boldness. Like Paul, may you be led by the Spirit, not by fear, and may your obedience produce eternal impact, in Jesus' name.

Let us pray

1. *Father, I thank You for Your faithfulness and for the gift of the Holy Spirit who gives me the power to obey You, in Jesus' name.*
2. *Father, give me boldness to stand alone when needed, and help me choose Your approval above human approval, in Jesus' name.*
3. *Father, strengthen me to endure trials without giving up on Your call over my life, in Jesus' name.*
4. *I break every spirit of fear—fear of death, rejection, and failure that tries to hold me back from full obedience, in Jesus' name.*
5. *I declare that my obedience will bear lasting fruit, and every decision led by Your Spirit will bring glory to Your name, in Jesus' name.*
6. *Nothing will stop me from doing God's will, in Jesus' name.*

DON'T DISHONOR YOUR PARENTS

Read: Ephesians 6:1-3

> **Bible in 1 year:** Ps. 127-132
> **Bible in 2 years:** Jonah 2-3

"Honor your father and your mother, so that you may live long in the land the LORD your God is giving you" (Exodus 20:12).

The Bible leaves no room for doubt about the danger of dishonoring our parents. In Deuteronomy 27:16, God warns, *"Cursed is anyone who dishonors their father or mother."* Similarly, Proverbs 20:20 states, *"If someone curses their father or mother, their lamp will be snuffed out in pitch darkness."* Such verses reveal that dishonoring parents brings serious consequences – spiritually, emotionally, and even physically.

Your parents are God's appointed authorities, entrusted to nurture, protect, and guide you. When you disrespect them, you not only dishonor them but also reject God's design for the family. In doing so, you open the door to destruction, loss, and spiritual blockages.

Consider Reuben, Jacob's firstborn. He dishonored his father by sleeping with his wife (Genesis 35:22). Later, Jacob declared over him: *"Unstable as water, you shall not excel..." (Genesis 49:4).* Reuben lost both his birthright and his leadership role. His story is a sobering reminder that dishonor toward parents can strip us of honor, blessings, and future inheritance.

If you are facing struggles, whether financial, relational, or spiritual, it is crucial to examine your relationship with your parents. Is all well? Humble yourself before God, seek forgiveness, and, where possible, reconcile with them. Remember: honoring your parents is not merely a commandment with a promise; it is a pathway to God's favor, peace, and blessing.

Let us pray

1. *Father, help me to honor and respect my parents in every word, thought, and action, in Jesus' name.*
2. *Lord, heal any bitterness or resentment between me and my parents, in Jesus' name.*
3. *Lord, grant me humility to seek forgiveness and reconciliation where I have caused hurt, in Jesus' name.*
4. *Father, break every generational curse and negative pattern caused by dishonor toward parents, in Jesus' name.*
5. *Father, fill my life with blessings, peace, and divine favor as I walk in obedience to Your command, in Jesus' name.*
6. *As the grace to honor my parents is restored in my life, every disgrace is wiped out, in Jesus' name.*

Sunday 30 November **STAY VIGILANT**

Read: Matthew 26:41

> **Bible in 1 year:** Ps.133-137
> **Bible in 2 years:** (Catch-Up)

"Therefore, let him who thinks he stands take heed lest he fall" (1 Corinthians 10:12).

Vigilance is absolutely essential for a victorious Christian life. After God has forgiven you of sin, don't open the door to the devil again. Remember: forgiveness does not make you immune to temptation; instead, it calls you to greater watchfulness. Sin often lurks at the door (Genesis 4:7), and without vigilance, even the strongest can stumble again.

The Greek word for 'Watch' (*Grēgoreō*) means "To be awake, alert, and on guard." Vigilance is a spiritual discipline – staying alert in prayer, sensitive to the Spirit, and cautious about environments that stir weakness.

Complacency is dangerous. David's fall with Bathsheba began when he lingered in comfort instead of leading in battle (2 Samuel 12). Likewise, when believers neglect prayer, worship, and obedience, they create openings for temptation. Restoration must be followed by renewed discipline, or the cycle repeats.

A city with repaired walls still needs guards at the gates. If the guards fall asleep, enemies can enter or scale the wall and undo all that was rebuilt. In the same way, restored believers must guard their eyes, thoughts, and choices with vigilance.

Vigilance is not fear; it is wisdom. We stay alert because we know the enemy is active. But we also stay hopeful, knowing God's Spirit empowers us to stand. With prayer, accountability, and God's Word, vigilance becomes a shield that keeps us walking in victory. Be vigilant!

Let us pray

1. *Father, keep me vigilant and prayerful every day, in Jesus' name.*
2. *Father, guard my heart and mind from the snares of the enemy, in Jesus' name.*
3. *Lord, deliver me from complacency and spiritual laziness, in Jesus' name.*
4. *Father, strengthen me to overcome temptation through Your Spirit, in Jesus' name.*
5. *Father, let me finish strong, standing firm till the end, in Jesus' name.*
6. *Father, You are my rock and my strength; I will not fall into the hands of my enemies, in Jesus' name.*

Monday 1 December   **LED BY THE CLOUD**

Read: Numbers 9:15-23

> **Bible in 1 year:** 2 Chron. 14-16
> **Bible in 2 years:** Jonah 4; Mic. 1

"I will instruct you and teach you in the way you should go; I will guide you with My eye" (Psalms 32:8).

Who leads you determines your destination. Satan wants you to follow the crowd, steering you away from God's plan for your life.

In Numbers 9:15-23, the Israelites followed the cloud by day and fire by night. Wherever it rested, they camped; when it moved, they moved. God's presence guided their journey, not popular opinion, comfort, or human plans. This cloud is a picture of the Holy Spirit, while the crowd represents worldly pressures – money, comfort, status, or ease.

In this life, many are driven by convenience or what everyone else is doing. But those who fulfill God's purpose learn to discern His voice and align their steps with His plan. True safety, prosperity, and impact are found at the center of God's will. Following God requires trust and courage.

A young IT engineer once received a call to a remote desert mission among an unreached people group. Logic and comfort said "No," but he obeyed. Today, many souls have been saved and churches planted. Following the crowd would have kept him safe but fruitless. Heaven values obedience and purpose, not wealth or popularity.

Like the Israelites, we must move when God moves, rest when He rests, and trust His timing. Kingdom resources, divine protection, and lasting impact come to those who follow the cloud, not the crowd.

Friend, if you want to experience God's best for your life, commit daily to His guidance, surrender your comfort, and choose His plan above all else. The best God has for you is always found in the center of His will.

Let us pray

1. *Father, thank You, for guiding me each day, in Jesus' name.*
2. *Father, help me hear and follow Your voice today and every day, in Jesus' name.*
3. *Father, give me courage to obey Your leading even when it's hard, in Jesus' name.*
4. *Father, keep me from following the crowd, in Jesus' name.*
5. *O Father, equip me to fulfill Your purpose and impact my generation, in Jesus' name.*
6. *I declare that this end of year, I will walk daily by God's guidance and prosper in all His ways, in Jesus' name.*

Prophetic Prayers of the Week

1. *"The Lord will bless the work of your hands"* (Deut. 28:12); *The works of my hand will prosper supernaturally this month, in Jesus' name.*
2. *"Weeping may last for the night, but joy comes in the morning"* (Ps. 30:5); *My morning of joy has come, in Jesus' name.*
3. *"Above all, clothe yourselves with love"* (Col. 3:14); *I receive the garment of God's love on my life today, in Jesus' name.*

Tuesday 2 December   **DON'T GIVE UP,**
                                LOOK UP

Read: Psalm 121:1-8

> **Bible in 1 year:** 2 Chron. 17-19
> **Bible in 2 years:** Mic. 2-3

"Looking unto Jesus the author and finisher of our faith; who for the joy that was set before him endured the cross, despising the shame, and is set down at the right hand of the throne of God" (Hebrews 12:2).

The direction of your look affects your heart and the outcome of your life. Scripture reminds us that our help does not come from within ourselves or from the world around us, but from the Lord Himself, above. So, don't give up, look up! Help will surely come!

If you look inward, you will quickly find discouragement. Human weakness, failure, and limitation can overwhelm your spirit. Left to ourselves, we are frail and imperfect, and this reality can rob us of hope.

If you look at the enemy, fear begins to rule your heart. Satan thrives on intimidation and manipulation. Like Peter walking on water, the moment you shift your focus to the storm, you begin to sink (Matthew 14:30). The enemy magnifies problems to make you forget God's promises. Perhaps you are sinking right now because you have focused so much on your problem.

But when you look upward to Christ, strength and encouragement flow. The psalmist reminds us that our help comes from the Lord, the Maker of heaven and earth. To

"Look up" is not just to glance; it means to *fix your gaze* with intention on the One who reigns above all. Hebrews 12:2 encourages you today to keep your eyes on Jesus, the Author and Finisher of your faith. He is faithful to intervene.

When I was learning to ride a bicycle, my teacher kept reminding me, "Don't look at the ground; keep your eyes forward." The moment I looked down, I lost balance, and guess what, I crashed on the ground. In the same way, when you, as a believer, look down at yourself or sideways at your fears, you stumble. But when they fix your gaze on Christ, stability comes.

So, friend, no matter what is going on in your life right now, don't give up; look up! God is your helper, your shield, and your victory. He will surely send you help.

Where you look will determine how you stand.

Let us pray

1. *Father, I thank You because You are my ever-present help and the lifter of my head, in Jesus' name.*
2. *O Lord, deliver me from self-reliance and help me to depend fully on You, in Jesus' name.*
3. *Lord Jesus, strengthen my faith to look beyond my fears and fix my eyes on You.*
4. *Father, arise and silence every voice of intimidation from the enemy that seeks to weaken my faith, in Jesus' name.*
5. *Lord, let Your Spirit remind me daily that my help comes from You alone, in Jesus' name.*
6. *I lift my eyes to the Lord; my help, my strength, and my victory come from Him alone, in Jesus' name.*

Wednesday 3 December　　　**A STRATEGY FOR YOUR FAMILY**

Read: Jeremiah 29:4-14

> **Bible in 1 year:** 2 Chron. 20-22
> **Bible in 2 years:** Mic. 4-5

"But seek first His kingdom and His righteousness, and all these things will be given to you as well" (Matthew 6:33 NIV).

God has a strategy for your family. He is never random – He is a God of strategy and purpose.

In Jeremiah 29, the exiles in Babylon longed for an immediate escape, but God told them to settle, build houses, plant gardens, marry, and multiply. He assured them, *"I know the plans I have for you... plans to prosper you and not to harm you, plans to give you hope and a future" (vs. 11).* The promise was wrapped in a process. Even in captivity, God had a strategy to preserve, grow, and prosper His people until His appointed time of deliverance.

Families must remember that God's blessings unfold step by step, not all at once. God's plan takes shape in our lives as we walk in discipline, wait with patience, and yield in obedience. Years ago, looking at my financial hardship, I asked the Lord, "Will I ever build a house for my family?" His answer was clear: "Yes, but follow My plan." At that time, my resources were limited, yet He led me step by step to buy small plots of land. Years later, we sold those plots and used the proceeds to build our home. That was not luck; it was God's strategy at work.

Jesus echoes the same principle in Matthew 6:33: when we seek first God's kingdom, divine order is released into every area of life, including family provision and stability. Strategies from heaven begin with alignment with God's will. Without His guidance, you risk gambling with your future.

Discipline, vision, and obedience are keys that activate God's plans. What begins small – like planting a seed can grow into a generational blessing when faithfully nurtured. Sit before God, receive His strategy, and walk it out step by step. His strategies always lead to fruitfulness, peace, and lasting success for your family.

Let us pray

1. *Father, thank You for having a good and intentional plan for my life and family, in Jesus' name.*
2. *Father, teach me to seek Your will and follow Your timing in every decision, in Jesus' name.*
3. *O Father, give me clarity, discipline, and boldness to walk in the strategy You reveal, in Jesus' name.*
4. *Father, break every cycle of stagnation, confusion, and wasted effort in my family, in Jesus' name.*
5. *O Lord, open our eyes to see opportunities that align with Your purpose for us, in Jesus' name.*
6. *I declare that my family shall walk in divine strategy, multiply in grace, and build generational legacy, in Jesus' name!*

Thursday 4 December   **LEARN FROM**
                             PEOPLE OF FAITH

Read: Hebrews 11:1-12

Bible in 1 year: 2 Chron.23-25
Bible in 2 years: Mic. 6-7

"Let us fix our eyes on Jesus, the author and perfecter of our faith..." (Hebrews 12:2 NIV).

God never intended for you to walk the journey of faith in isolation. The Bible is filled with men and women whose lives still inspire us today. Abraham trusted God for a promised son and waited decades to see it fulfilled. Joseph endured rejection, betrayal, and prison before stepping into his destiny. Moses bore the weight of leading a rebellious people through the wilderness. Yet, he persevered because he *"saw Him who is invisible" (Hebrews 11:27).* The writer of Hebrews reminds us that their faith still speaks, echoing across generations as a testimony of God's faithfulness (Hebrews 11:4).

But learning from faith does not stop at Scripture. God continues to write living testimonies through believers around us. Years ago, I listened to a young couple share how God enabled them to buy land. Only a year later, they returned with a testimony of purchasing their first home. At that time, I had been in ministry for twelve years, faithfully serving yet owning no land. Though their story challenged me, it did not discourage me. It ignited a spark of faith in my heart. As I prayed, God whispered, *"You too can build, if you follow My plan."* That moment taught me that testimonies are

92

not for comparison but for inspiration. I followed his plan and got a home for my family.

Hebrews 12:2 calls us to fix our eyes on Jesus, the ultimate model of endurance. He endured the cross, despising its shame, and now sits at the right hand of God. When we learn from others, both from the pages of Scripture and from present-day witnesses, we are reminded that God's promises are worth waiting for, His plans are worth trusting, and His strategies are worth following.

Surround your family with stories of faith. Let the testimony of those who endured and overcame become fuel for your own journey. Their victories point to the God who is still faithful today.

Let us pray

1. *Father, thank You for the cloud of witnesses who inspire and challenge us to persevere, in Jesus' name.*
2. *Help me to learn from the faith of others and grow stronger in my own walk, in Jesus' name.*
3. *Father, let my family be surrounded by people whose lives reflect Your faithfulness, in Jesus' name.*
4. *Father, deliver us from comparison, discouragement, and jealousy; fill us with godly inspiration, in Jesus' name.*
5. *Father, give us discernment to receive wisdom and direction through the testimonies of others, in Jesus' name.*
6. *I declare that my family shall walk in multiplied grace, fueled by testimonies and anchored in faith, in Jesus' name!*

Friday 5 December **STICK TO THE PLAN**

Read: Nehemiah 4:1-9

Bible in 1 year: 2 Chron. 26-29
Bible in 2 years: Nah. 1-2

I have come down from heaven not to do my will but to do the will of him who sent me" (John 6:38 NIV).

Starting strong is easy, but finishing well requires determination. Nehemiah was given a divine assignment: to rebuild Jerusalem's broken walls. His enemies mocked, threatened, and tried to distract him, but Nehemiah refused to quit. With prayer on his lips and a sword in one hand, he kept working until the task was complete (Nehemiah 4:17-18). His perseverance reshaped the destiny of a nation.

Jesus Himself is our perfect example of staying true to God's plan. He declared in John 6:38, *"I have come down from heaven not to do my will but to do the will of him who sent me."* Even when the agony of the cross stood before Him, He pressed forward in obedience. Real perseverance is not stubbornness; it is unwavering obedience to the will of God.

The Greek word for *"Will"* here is *'Theléma,'* meaning God's deliberate purpose or intention. To follow His will is to align your steps with His eternal design, even when it costs you.

In life, God often gives a plan that begins with joy and excitement. Yet as time passes, obstacles arise – critics mock, delays frustrate, and doubts whisper, "Did God really say this?" That is when your faith is tested.

I recall the time God gave me a strategy to buy small plots of land, despite our limited income. While others were already building houses, we were still saving. At times, it felt slow and discouraging, but we stuck to the plan. Years later, those plots became the key to building our family home. That journey taught me never to abandon God's strategy because of pressure or delay.

When God speaks, His word is sure. Stick to what He said, and in His time, He will bring it to completion.

Let us pray

1. *Father, thank You for every divine plan You have given me and my family, in Jesus' name.*
2. *Father, strengthen our resolve to stay focused on the purpose You've laid before us, in Jesus' name.*
3. *Father, silence every voice of fear, distraction, or discouragement in our path, in Jesus' name.*
4. *O Lord, teach us the discipline to obey Your instructions even when results seem delayed, in Jesus' name.*
5. *Father, let our hearts remain steadfast and our hands diligent until we see the promise fulfilled, in Jesus' name.*
6. *I declare that our family shall complete every assignment, fulfill every vision, and reap every harvest, in Jesus' name!*

Saturday 6 December **GOD IS FAITHFUL, TRUST HIM**

Read: Lamentations 3:22-23

> **Bible in 1 year:** 2 Chron. 30-32
> **Bible in 2 years:** Nah. 3; Hab. 1

"God is faithful, by whom you were called into the fellowship of his Son, Jesus Christ our Lord" (1 Corinthians 1:9).

In a world marked by instability and betrayal, it is deeply reassuring to know that God is faithful. His faithfulness is not dependent on our goodness, strength, or even our belief. It is rooted in His unchanging character.

The word "Faithful" in Hebrew is *'Emunah,'* and in Greek it is *'Pistos.'* It conveys firmness, reliability, loyalty, and constancy. This means God is not just someone who occasionally does what He says; He is someone who never fails to do what He has promised. He is faithful by nature, not just by action.

When life seems to contradict God's promises, when your prayers are delayed, and you feel like losing hope, don't worry about understanding what is happening; trust God's heart. He is faithful! He cannot lie.

The prophet Jeremiah wrote Lamentations while mourning the destruction of Jerusalem. Yet in the middle of his grief, he declared, *"Great is Your faithfulness."* That wasn't a feeling. That was a decision to trust God in the darkest hour. Can you still trust God after all you have gone through so far?

96

Christ is the greatest proof of God's faithfulness. Every prophecy about the Messiah was fulfilled in Jesus. His birth (Isaiah 7:14), His death (Isaiah 53), and His resurrection (Psalm 16:10). These are not just stories; they are evidence that God keeps His Word, no matter how long it takes or how impossible it seems.

Imagine a farmer who plants seeds in barren soil. Day after day, he waters them, though he sees no growth. Why? Because he trusts the process. Likewise, you may not see the result of your prayers immediately, but the faithfulness of God guarantees that His promises will bear fruit in due time. Trust Him. He is faithful!

Let us pray

1. *Father, thank You for Your constant and unfailing faithfulness in every season of my life.*
2. *Father, I place my confidence in Your promises, knowing You are not a man that You should lie.*
3. *O Lord, revive my heart in times of waiting, and remind me that You are always working.*
4. *Father, teach me to wait patiently, anchored in Your Word and not my emotions.*
5. *Father, help me keep my eyes on Christ, the living proof of Your covenant-keeping nature.*
6. *I boldly declare that every promise of God over my life shall be fulfilled without delay or failure, for great is His faithfulness, in Jesus' name.*

Sunday 7 December   **GOD'S WORD IS FINAL**

Read: Isaiah 54:13-17

> **Bible in 1 year:** Job 1-4
> **Bible in 2 years:** Hab. 2-3

"God is not a man, that He should lie, nor a son of man, that He should change His mind. Does He speak and then not act? Does He promise and not fulfill?" (Numbers 23:19 NIV).

No man can change what God has said about you. The people of this world may engage in manipulation, injustice, and demonic opposition against you. Wicked people may set up visible or invisible embargoes against you. They may use corrupt systems, twisted laws, and even spiritual forces to try to delay or destroy what God has ordained for you. But take heart: man's verdict is not God's final word. All their plans against you will fail, in Jesus' name.

In Numbers 23:20, the prophet Balaam, though hired to curse Israel, declared, *"He has blessed, and I cannot reverse it."* The Hebrew word for "Reverse" here implies to *undo, cancel, or make void.* Once God commands a blessing, no force can revoke it. His Word is unchallengeable in every court, natural or spiritual.

The Bible gives clear examples of people using God's Word and divine alignment to overturn evil decrees. In Esther 8, Haman's wicked law was set to destroy the Jews. But Esther, through prayer and boldness, moved the king to issue another decree that gave God's people the right to fight back. In Daniel 6, a law was passed forbidding prayer, but Daniel chose God over compromise, and God overruled that decree by delivering him from the lions' den.

The Word of God serves as your legal authority to overcome every negative word, curse, or manipulation. Isaiah 54:17 affirms, *"No weapon formed against you shall prosper, and every tongue that rises against you in judgment, you shall condemn."* This is not wishful thinking; it is covenant language.

Imagine a seal on a royal decree. Once stamped, only the king can change it. God's stamp is on your destiny, and no one else holds that authority to reverse it. You are blessed! Don't surrender to the lies of Satan. It shall be well with you, in Jesus' name.

Let us pray

1. *Father, thank You because Your Word over my life is final and irreversible.*
2. *Father, empower me to stand on Your promises when the world speaks otherwise, in Jesus' name.*
3. *Father, help me detect and reject every evil decree spoken against me, in Jesus' name.*
4. *Lord, let my life align with Your voice and not the lies of the enemy, in Jesus' name.*
5. *Father, teach me to speak Your Word with confidence to overturn every wicked plan of Satan, in Jesus' name.*
6. *I decree that every contrary voice and wicked law working against my life is cancelled by the power of the Word and the blood,* **in Jesus' name.**

Monday 8 December   **ARE YOU TIRED OF GOD?**

Read: Isaiah 40:25-31

> **Bible in 1 year:** Job 5-7
> **Bible in 2 years:** Zeph. 1-2

"O My people, what have I done to you? What have I done to make you tired of Me? Answer Me!" (Micah 6:3 NLT).

Spiritual tiredness is real. It's not just fatigue in the body; it's a weariness that settles in the soul. When you've believed God, prayed, served, endured hardship, and yet feel like the breakthrough is still far away, your heart can grow faint. Discouragement creeps in subtly. You may still attend church, sing the songs, and say the words, but deep inside, you've grown tired of God. Tired of waiting, tired of trying, tired of believing.

In Micah 6, God doesn't rebuke His people with anger; instead, He asks them a question filled with compassion: *"What have I done to make you tired of Me?" (vs. 3).* Then He gently reminds them: *"I brought you out of Egypt, I redeemed you, I protected you, I guided you" (vs. 4).* God is not unaware of your burdens; He wants to bring your focus back to His faithfulness.

The Hebrew word for "Tired" in our main verse suggests a soul worn out from struggle. But God doesn't condemn weariness; He offers strength. Isaiah 40:29-31 promises that He gives power to the faint and renews the strength of those who wait on Him. To "Wait" here means to bind together, to cling to God in hope and trust. It is not passive, but persistent. He doesn't ask you to perform; He asks you to lean on Him.

Imagine a child too tired to walk, resting in the arms of a strong father. That's how God wants you to trust Him again. He is not angry with your weariness; He wants to restore you.

Let us pray

1. *Father, I thank You for Your patience and mercy toward me even when my heart has grown tired, in Jesus' name.*
2. *Father, forgive me for allowing discouragement and pressure to rob me of intimacy with You, in Jesus' name.*
3. *Father, please fill me again with fresh fire, fresh hunger, and fresh passion for Your presence, in Jesus' name.*
4. *Lord, open my eyes to see how far You've brought me, and remind me of the miracles I've already witnessed, in Jesus' name.*
5. *Help me to wait on You with renewed expectation, trusting that You are still working even when I don't feel it, in Jesus' name.*
6. *I declare that my strength is being renewed, and I will rise again with divine energy and spiritual fire,* **in Jesus' name.**

Prophetic Prayers of the Week

1. *"You will tread on the lion and the cobra"* (Ps. 91:13); *I crush demonic powers underfoot, in Jesus' name.*
2. *"The snare is broken, and we have escaped"* (Ps. 124:7); *I escape every satanic trap this month, in Jesus' name.*
3. *"Be still and know that I am God"* (Ps. 46:10); *I remain unshaken in any storm this month, in Jesus' name.*

Tuesday 9 December **ROOTING OUT**
                              GIANTS

Read: Joshua 15:13-16

> **Bible in 1 year:** Job 8-10
> **Bible in 2 years:** Zeph. 3; Hag. 1

"Caleb drove out from there three Anakites – Sheshai, Ahiman, and Talmai, the descendants of Anak" (Joshua 15:14 NET).

Divine open doors come with adversaries (1 Corinthians 16:9). You need the mindset of a warrior to possess your possession.

When Caleb claimed Hebron, he did not inherit an empty city. It was occupied by giants – the descendants of Anak, mighty men who had terrified Israel 45 years earlier (Numbers 13:28). Yet Caleb, at 85 years old, was ready to root them out. He believed the same God who had promised the land would empower him to conquer it. You need such determination to take the territory God has given you. Don't back off because of fear.

Giants often guard our promised places. Sheshai (whitish, noble) points to pride and self-righteousness that blinds us. Ahiman (brother of the right hand) represents false alliances and misplaced confidence. Talmai (abounding in furrows, ridges) suggests deeply entrenched systems or generational strongholds. These giants symbolize barriers – fear, sin, doubt, addictions, and family cycles that try to keep us from expansion in Christ.

But Christ has already secured our victory. On the cross, He disarmed principalities and powers (Colossians 2:15). Through Him, we overcome the giants of our generation. Caleb's courage mirrors Paul's declaration: *"In all these things we are more than conquerors through Him who loved us"* (Romans 8:37).

There was a young believer who feared pursuing higher studies because no one in his family had ever gone to college. That generational "Giant" of limitation kept him bound. But when he trusted God, applied in faith, and received a scholarship, he became the first in his family to graduate. He broke the cycle and opened doors for others.

As a believer, you are called like Caleb to drive out giants so that generations after you can inherit freedom. Giants may look strong, but the promises of God are stronger. With faith, patience, and courage in Christ, you will root out the giants in your territory and stand in your Hebron, in Jesus' name.

Let us pray
1. *Father, thank You for giving me victory in Christ over every giant, in Jesus' name.*
2. *Lord, open my eyes to recognize the giants occupying my inheritance, in Jesus' name.*
3. *By the power of the cross, I uproot every giant of fear, pride, and doubt in my life, in Jesus' name.*
4. *Father, arise and break every generational stronghold or limitation resisting my expansion, in Jesus' name.*
5. *Father, empower me with Caleb's spirit of faith and courage to take my Hebron, in Jesus' name.*
6. *I declare: Every giant must fall, and I will possess my inheritance in Christ, in Jesus' name.*

103

Wednesday 10 December   **PRIORITIZE YOUR LIFE**

Read: Luke 10:38-42

> **Bible in 1 year:** Job 11-13
> **Bible in 2 years:** Hag. 2; Zech. 1

"But seek first his kingdom and his righteousness, and all these things will be given to you as well" (Matthew 6:33).

Life is full of demands, distractions, and countless responsibilities. Yet Scripture teaches that not everything carries the same weight. Some things are urgent, others are important, but only a few are eternal. Jesus gives us the principle of priorities: *"Seek first the kingdom of God and His righteousness" (Matthew 6:33).* What we place first shapes the rest of our lives. It is like buttoning your shirt. Everything flows nicely when the first button is done correctly. But when you miss the first button, everything loses shape.

When priorities are misplaced, confusion follows. Martha busied herself with preparations for Jesus while Mary sat at His feet (Luke 10:38-42). Jesus affirmed that Mary had chosen *"The one thing that is necessary."* Solomon, though endowed with wisdom, pursued wealth, pleasure, and alliances with foreign kings above devotion to God, which led to his downfall (1 Kings 11:1-6). On the other hand, Paul declared, *"This one thing I do: forgetting what is behind and straining toward what is ahead, I press on toward the goal..." (Philippians 3:13-14).* His singular focus enabled him to finish well.

Prioritizing your life means aligning your time, energy, and resources with what truly matters: God's kingdom, relationships, and eternal values. It means saying no to distractions, avoiding busyness that bears no fruit, and choosing quality over quantity. Even rest is a godly priority, as Jesus Himself withdrew to pray and refresh (Mark 1:35).

Beloved, you cannot be everywhere or do everything, but you can choose to do what matters most. A life of misplaced priorities wastes potential; a life of godly priorities fulfills destiny. Start each day asking: *What comes first in God's eyes today? Do everything in order.*

Let us pray

1. *Father, I thank You for giving me clarity through Your Word to know what matters most, in Jesus' name.*
2. *Lord, forgive me for every time I have misplaced priorities and pursued vanity over Your kingdom, in Jesus' name.*
3. *Father, give me wisdom and discipline to align my daily choices with eternal values, in Jesus' name.*
4. *Lord, help me to invest my time, resources, and energy in things that glorify You, in Jesus' name.*
5. *Father, remove every distraction that pulls me away from seeking You first, in Jesus' name.*
6. *I declare that my life is aligned with God's priorities; I will seek first His kingdom, and all other things shall follow, in Jesus' name.*

Thursday 11 December   **BREAKING A
                              SATANIC
                              COALITION**

Read: Joshua 11:1-7

> **Bible in 1 year:** Job 14-17
> **Bible in 2 years:** Zech. 2-3

*"Then the LORD said to Joshua, 'Do not be afraid of
them, because by this time tomorrow I will hand all of
them, slain, over to Israel. You are to hamstring their
horses and burn their chariots'" (Joshua 11:6 NIV).*

S atan fights us through evil coalitions. He understands
the impact of synergy in warfare.

When Israel advanced into their inheritance,
King Jabin of Hazor formed a coalition of kings to fight
against them. Hazor, meaning "Fortified," points to
entrenched powers. Jobab means "Wail of tribulation," a
picture of oppression. Achshaph means "Sorcery," showing
the demonic nature of the opposition. These names reveal
that satanic coalitions are not accidental; they are intentional
alliances designed to frustrate God's people.

Satan still forms coalitions today to stop believers
from fulfilling their God-given assignments. These may
appear as coordinated attacks – fear, oppression, sorcery, or
systemic barriers. Yet God's Word to Joshua was clear: *"Do
not be afraid of them."* The Lord Himself promised to deliver
the coalition into Israel's hands. Likewise, Christ has already
disarmed powers and principalities through His victory on
the cross (Colossians 2:15).

106

Joshua responded with boldness by launching a sudden attack near Merom (Joshua 11:7). Delay would have given the coalition more strength, but immediate obedience brought victory. Similarly, believers must confront satanic resistance without hesitation, through fervent prayer, bold faith, and obedience to God's Word.

A strong biblical example is Nehemiah. When rebuilding Jerusalem's walls, he faced a coalition of Sanballat, Tobiah, and Geshem (Nehemiah 4:7-9). They mocked, threatened, and plotted together to stop the work. Yet Nehemiah armed the builders with prayer, watchfulness, and perseverance. The coalition failed because God's people stayed focused and obedient.

Whenever satanic coalitions rise against you, it is a sign that your progress threatens the enemy. Stand firm in Christ, fear not, confront them in faith, and victory will surely be yours.

Let us pray

1. *Father, thank You for assuring me of victory over every satanic alliance, in Jesus' name.*

2. *Lord, expose and scatter every coalition raised against my life and assignment, in Jesus' name.*

3. *Father, strengthen me to resist fear and intimidation with bold faith, in Jesus' name.*

4. *Father, arise and break the hold of sorcery, enchantments, and manipulations set against me, in Jesus' name.*

5. *Father, grant me grace to walk in obedience so I may enjoy Your divine backing, in Jesus' name.*

6. *I declare: Every satanic coalition is broken, and I advance in unstoppable victory, in Jesus' name.*

Friday 12 December　　　　**RESULT CANCELS**
　　　　　　　　　　　　　　　　　INSULT

Read: Numbers 17:1-13

> **Bible in 1 year:** Job 18-20
> **Bible in 2 years:** Zech. 4-5

"Now it came to pass on the next day that Moses went into the tabernacle of witness, and behold, the rod of Aaron, of the house of Levi, had sprouted and put forth buds, had produced blossoms and yielded ripe almonds" (Numbers 17:8).

God delights in defending those He has chosen. When Aaron's priesthood was questioned, God commanded that every tribe bring forth a rod. By morning, Aaron's rod had not only budded but also blossomed and produced ripe almonds. Overnight, God validated Aaron's calling with undeniable results.

This miracle shows us that divine choice is not proved by arguments but by fruit. Criticism and insults may surround your life or ministry, but when God releases results, every mouth is silenced. The resurrection power that caused a dead stick to bear fruit is the same power working in you through Christ. Paul affirms: *"The Spirit of Him who raised Jesus from the dead dwells in you" (Romans 8:11).* Don't be intimidated by anybody.

Aaron's experience teaches us that insults cannot cancel God's calling, but results born of His power will cancel insults. When God's hand is on you, He will manifest miracles that human reasoning cannot deny. Like Jesus' critics, who accused Him relentlessly, even they had to confess, *"What shall we do? For this man works many miracles"* *(John 11:47)*. May God disprove your critics and adversaries with supernatural results, in Jesus' name!

A brother in Christ who was despised and mocked in his workplace for his faith began praying for his colleagues. Soon, testimonies of healing and breakthrough emerged, and those who mocked him began to seek his prayers. The results spoke louder than the insults.

No matter how "Dead" a situation seems, whether family, health, or calling, God can release fruit overnight. When His resurrection power works through you, results will testify, and insults will fade away.

Let us pray
1. *Father, thank You for choosing and defending me through Christ, in Jesus' name.*
2. *Lord, let every dead area of my life blossom by Your resurrection power, in Jesus' name.*
3. *Father, silence every voice of accusation against my calling with undeniable results, in Jesus' name.*
4. *Father, release miracles in my family, ministry, and community that cancel every insult, in Jesus' name.*
5. *O Lord, empower me to walk in the authority of Christ and bear lasting fruit, in Jesus' name.*
6. *I declare: The resurrection power of Christ is at work in me; results will cancel every insult, in Jesus' name.*

ANNOUNCEMENT
*Prepare for the **ANNUAL PRAYER AND FASTING DAY** for **PRAYER STORM** on Friday, 19 December 2025. Theme: **ANOTHER LEVEL***

**RESPONDING TO
THREATENING
MESSAGES**

Read: Nehemiah 4:10-14

Bible in 1 year: Job 21-24
Bible in 2 years: Zech. 6-7

"After I looked things over, I stood up and said to the nobles, the officials, and the rest of the people, 'Don't be afraid of them. Remember the Lord, who is great and awesome, and fight for your families, your sons and your daughters, your wives and your homes'" *(Nehemiah 4:14 NIV).*

When Nehemiah and the Jews rebuilt Jerusalem's walls, their enemies issued repeated threats: *"Before they know it, we will kill them and put an end to the work"* (v.11). These threats spread quickly, echoed even by fellow Jews who repeated the warnings ten times (v.12). Threats have a way of multiplying through voices, visions, and repeated bad reports. The goal is simple: to wear you down mentally and stop you from advancing.

"Threat" in Hebrew is *'yare'*, meaning "To frighten, cause fear, or terrorize." Threats are weapons of intimidation designed to weaken courage and stop progress. Satan uses threats because fear is one of his strongest weapons. He cannot stop God's plan, but he wants you to stop yourself through discouragement. Elijah, though a mighty prophet, ran into despair when Jezebel threatened him (1 Kings 19:2–3). The threat was only words, but it shook him deeply.

110

How then do we respond? Nehemiah shows us four keys. First, he trusted in God's greatness: *"Remember the Lord, who is great and awesome"* (v.14). Confidence in God's power dismantles fear. Second, he encouraged the people, speaking faith in the face of fear. Third, he armed them with swords, spears, and bows; reminding us to be spiritually armed with prayer, Scripture, and faith (Ephesians 6:10-17). Finally, he mobilized corporate action; families stood together, united against the enemy. The result? God frustrated the enemy's plans, and the people returned to work (v.15).

This man received a medical report from the hospital that traumatized him. But when he chose to stand on God's Word and surrounded himself with praying friends, fear gave way to peace, and healing followed.

What threat is Satan trying to use to break your courage? Friend, remember who your God is. Stand, armed in faith, and unite with others. The enemy's plots against you will be frustrated.

Let us pray

1. *Father, thank You for being greater than every threat against my life, in Jesus' name.*
2. *Lord, silence every voice of intimidation and fear raised against me, in Jesus' name.*
3. *O Father, strengthen my heart to remember Your greatness and power, in Jesus' name.*
4. *Father, arm me with Your Word, prayer, and faith to withstand the enemy, in Jesus' name.*
5. *Father, unite my family, church, and community to stand together against evil schemes, in Jesus' name.*
6. *I declare: Every satanic threat against me is frustrated; I will continue and prosper in my God-given assignment, in Jesus' name.*

PROPHESYING BY AN EVIL SPIRIT

Read: 2 Corinthians 11:3-4, 13-15

> **Bible in 1 year:** Job 25-27
>
> **Bible in 2 years:** Zech. 8-9

"The next day, an evil spirit from God rushed upon Saul, and he prophesied within his house. Now David was playing the lyre that day. There was a spear in Saul's hand" (1 Samuel 18:10 NET.

Not every prophecy comes from the Holy Spirit. That is why Scripture warns us to test the spirits (1 John 4:1).

Saul is a sobering example. Once anointed by God, he later opened doors to disobedience and jealousy. When the Spirit of the Lord departed from him (1 Samuel 16:14), an evil spirit came upon him, and he began to prophesy under its influence. Outwardly, it looked spiritual, but the source was corrupted.

This teaches us a vital lesson: it is not the beauty or excitement of the message that validates prophecy, but the spirit behind it. Evil-inspired prophecy often leads to confusion, deviation from truth, and strange doctrines. Its goal is to pollute faith and entrap believers. Paul warns in our text that even Satan can disguise himself as an angel of light (2 Corinthians 11:14).

How then can we discern? First, check alignment with God's Word. True prophecy will exalt Christ and align with Scripture (Revelation 19:10). Second, examine the fruit: does it produce holiness, love, and obedience? Jesus said, *'By their fruits you will know them*" (Matthew 7:16). Third, test the spirit in prayer, asking God for discernment. The Holy Spirit never contradicts Himself.

A church once welcomed a "Prophet" whose messages excited crowds, but over time, his words produced division, fear, and manipulation. When leaders tested the source, it was clear he was operating under a wrong spirit. Once the church renounced the spirit and prayed, peace was restored.

As a believer, you must not celebrate every voice but carefully discern. In these last days, demonic deception is on the increase, but those rooted in Christ will not be led astray. Hold fast to the Word, be filled with the Spirit, and test every prophecy.

Let us pray

1. *Father, thank You for giving me the Holy Spirit as the Spirit of truth, in Jesus' name.*
2. *Lord, grant me discernment to test the spirits behind every prophecy, in Jesus' name.*
3. *Father, deliver me from deception, manipulation, and strange doctrines, in Jesus' name.*
4. *Father, arise, let every evil-inspired voice assigned to derail me be silenced, in Jesus' name.*
5. *Father, fill me with Your Word and Spirit so I can rightly discern truth, in Jesus' name.*
6. *I declare: I will not be deceived—only the voice of the Holy Spirit shall guide me, in Jesus' name.*

Monday 15 December　　　　**SATAN WANTS YOU BLIND**

Read: 2 Corinthians 4:1-5

> **Bible in 1 year:** Ps. 82-84
> **Bible in 2 years:** Zech. 10-11

"The god of this age has blinded the minds of unbelievers, so that they cannot see the light of the gospel that displays the glory of Christ, who is the image of God" (2 Corinthians 4:4 NIV).

To be blind spiritually is to be vulnerable to satanic torment. That is why Satan wants you blind.

In 1 Samuel 11, Nahash the Ammonite demanded to gouge out the right eye of Israel's men as the price for peace. His strategy was cruel but revealing: he knew that blindness would weaken them, humiliate them, and make them vulnerable. Likewise, Satan seeks to blind God's people spiritually so they cannot perceive truth, resist deception, or walk in victory.

"Blind" in Greek is *'Typhloō,'* meaning "To obscure vision, to darken, or to make unable to perceive." Spiritual blindness is the inability to discern truth, caused by sin, deception, or hardness of heart. Blindness renders one vulnerable. Samson, once a mighty deliverer, became a grinder in a Philistine prison the moment his eyes were taken out (Judges 16:21). The enemy knows that if he blinds your vision, your strength is wasted. Blindness also renders one unproductive. Jesus said, *"If the blind lead the blind, both will fall into a pit"* (Matthew 15:14). Without vision, even strong people stumble.

114

What causes spiritual blindness? Sin darkens the heart (Ephesians 4:18), pride blinds the mind (John 9:41), and false teaching clouds discernment (2 Peter 2:1). Satan especially uses deception, false doctrines, immorality, and distractions to obscure the light of Christ.

How then do we protect our spiritual sight? First, through the Word of God, which enlightens our eyes (Psalm 19:8). Second, by the Spirit of wisdom and revelation, which opens the eyes of our hearts (Ephesians 1:17-18). Third, by living in purity and obedience. Sin tolerated is sight diminished.

A man confessed that immoral living led to a physical disease that cost him his eyesight. This story reminds us that spiritual blindness also begins when sin is tolerated. So, guard your vision. Treasure the light of God's Word. Stay filled with the Spirit. Refuse compromise. For when your eyes see clearly, you walk securely in the will of God.

Let us pray

1. *Father, thank You for opening my eyes to the light of Christ, in Jesus' name.*

2. *Lord, protect me from every form of spiritual blindness, in Jesus' name.*

3. *Remove pride, sin, and deception that seek to darken my vision, in Jesus' name.*

4. *Father, open the eyes of my heart by Your Spirit, that I may know Your will, in Jesus' name.*

5. *Father, preserve my spiritual sight through Your Word and purity, in Jesus' name.*

6. *I declare: My eyes are open; I will see, discern, and walk in God's light, in Jesus' name.*

Prophetic Prayers of the Week

1. *"No weapon formed against you shall prosper"* (Isa. 54:17); *Satan's weapons are powerless against my family and me, in Jesus' name.*

2. *"Those who wait on the Lord renew strength"* (Isa. 40:31); *My strength is renewed this morning, in Jesus' name.*

3. *"Be strong and courageous"* (Josh. 1:9); *I step out today with divine courage for supernatural results, in Jesus' name.*

Tuesday 16 December   **PRAY FOR YOUR MARRIAGE**

Read: Ecclesiastes 4:9-12

> **Bible in 1 year:** Ps. 85-86
> **Bible in 2 years:** Zech. 12-13

"Again, truly I tell you that if two of you on earth agree about anything they ask for, it will be done for them by my Father in heaven" (Matthew 18:19 NIV).

Prayer is the oxygen of a thriving marriage. Research shows that while nearly half of marriages end in divorce, fewer than one percent of couples who pray together daily end their marriage. This highlights a powerful truth: couples who unite before God in prayer invite His presence into their relationship, and His presence sustains them.

The word *"Agree" in Matthew 18:19* is Greek '*Symphōneō*,' which means "To sound together, to be in harmony." Prayer in marriage is not just about words but about uniting hearts in harmony before God.

Why don't many couples pray together? Some struggle with different prayer styles; one prays long, the other short. Others face constant interruptions from children, work, or distractions. For some, prayer feels awkward or forced. Yet the problem is not difficulty, but inconsistency. The enemy knows that a praying couple is a strong couple, so he fights to keep them silent.

Daniel prayed three times daily even under threat (Daniel 6:10). If he could maintain discipline under persecution, surely couples can build a rhythm of prayer in their homes. Prayer together is more than asking for needs; it's uniting hearts, resolving conflicts, and declaring God's promises over the family. Ecclesiastes 4:12 reminds us, *"A cord of three strands is not quickly broken."*

When husband, wife, and Christ are united in prayer, the marriage is fortified. A couple testified that, despite frequent arguments, committing to pray together each night, even briefly, deepened their intimacy. Petty conflicts lost their power, and love grew stronger. Prayer didn't just change their circumstances; it changed their hearts.

Couples who pray together daily discover that prayer is not just a spiritual duty but a relational glue. Start simple, be consistent, and trust God to strengthen your bond.

Let us pray

1. *Father, thank You for the gift of marriage and the power of praying together, in Jesus' name.*
2. *Lord, teach us as a couple to agree in prayer and walk in unity, in Jesus' name.*
3. *Father, remove every distraction and inconsistency that hinders prayer in our marriage, in Jesus' name.*
4. *Let prayer be the foundation of intimacy, strength, and direction in our home, in Jesus' name.*
5. *Father, cover our marriage with Your presence and protect it from the attacks of the enemy, in Jesus' name.*
6. *I declare: Our marriage will be prayerful, powerful, and unbreakable in Christ, in Jesus' name.*

Wednesday 17 December   **BREAK THE CYCLE**
                              OF FINANCIAL LACK

Read: Malachi 3:8-11

> **Bible in 1 year:** Ps. 87-88
> **Bible in 2 years:** Zech. 14

"But seek first the kingdom of God and his righteousness, and all these things will be provided for you" (Matthew 6:33).

Financial lack is not always about money; it is often about misplaced priorities. Many believers remain trapped in cycles of debt, worry, and insufficiency because they treat money as a purely material issue when, in reality, it is spiritual.

Jesus taught, *"Seek first the kingdom of God and His righteousness, and all these things will be provided for you" (Matthew 6:33).* When God is not first in our finances, we experience disorder. But when He is first, the cycle of lack is broken.

The principle of the tithe is central. Malachi 3:10 says, *"Bring the whole tithe into the storehouse, that there may be food in my house. Test me in this... and see if I will not throw open the floodgates of heaven and pour out so much blessing..."* The tithe is not just a donation; it is an act of covenant obedience. It acknowledges that God owns it all, and it positions us to receive His blessing.

Generosity is God's strategy for breaking cycles of lack. Proverbs 11:24 reminds us: *"One person gives freely, yet gains even more; another withholds unduly, but comes to poverty."* The world says, "Keep more to have more." God says, "Give, and it will be given to you" (Luke 6:38).

119

A Christian man testified that, though he struggled financially, he decided to tithe faithfully. At first, it felt impossible, but as he rearranged his life to put God first, doors of provision began opening. Over time, the cycle of lack broke, and he became a channel of blessing to others.

If you want to break financial lack, put God first. Rearrange your life around Him, not around bills, wants, or fears. Generosity is not subtraction; it's multiplication in God's economy.

Let us pray

1. *Father, thank You for being my source and provider, in Jesus' name.*
2. *Lord, deliver me from fear and unbelief in the area of finances, in Jesus' name.*
3. *Father, teach me to put You first and honor You with my tithe and offerings, in Jesus' name.*
4. *I break every cycle of financial lack and insufficiency in my life, in Jesus' name.*
5. *Father, make me a channel of blessing to my family, church, and community, in Jesus' name.*
6. *I declare: I am free from financial lack; God is first, and abundance follows, in Jesus' name.*

Thursday 18 December   **YOU CAN LOVE AGAIN**

Read: Ephesians 4:26-32

> **Bible in 1 year:** Ps. 89-90
> **Bible in 2 years:** Mal. 1-2

"Lay aside bitter words, temper tantrums, revenge, profanity, and insults. But instead, be kind and affectionate toward one another. Has God graciously forgiven you? Then graciously forgive one another in the depths of Christ's love" (Ephesians 4:31-32 TPT).

Marriage thrives on love, and love cannot exist without forgiveness. *"Forgive"* in Greek is *'Charizomai,'* which means "To show grace, to freely give, to pardon." Forgiveness is the soil in which love can grow again.

When bitterness, suspicion, or betrayal creep in, the fountain of love begins to dry. Yet the gospel reminds us that the love of Christ forgives, restores, and rekindles hope. If God has graciously forgiven us, then we also can forgive one another in the depths of His love (Ephesians 4:32).

What kills love in marriage?
Absence, neglect of responsibilities, accusations, unfaithfulness, and uncontrolled anger. These are love-killers that weaken intimacy and destroy trust. Over time, they produce poor communication, emotional coldness, and a dying marriage. When prayer and affection disappear, the bond slowly fades.

But no marriage is beyond repair if Christ is invited in. Just as Jesus turned water into wine at Cana (John 2:1-

11), He can turn bitterness into sweetness and restore love where it has run dry. The first step is **DESIRE** – a willingness to try again. Then comes **DECISION** – **ch**oosing to forgive, rebuild, and recommit. For those who have fallen into sin, **DELIVERANCE** through repentance and cleansing is vital. Love can be demanded of God, for He alone pours His love into our hearts by the Holy Spirit (Romans 5:5).

Many couples testify that when they reintroduced prayer, dialogue, and discipline into their home, love began to flow again. Setting boundaries, spending time together, and practicing daily kindness reopened the fountain of affection.

If your marriage feels dry, don't give up. You can love again. The God who resurrects the dead can resurrect your home.

Let us pray

1. *Father, thank You for Your unfailing love and forgiveness that sustains my life, in Jesus' name.*
2. *Lord, uproot every bitterness, anger, or accusation draining love in my marriage, in Jesus' name.*
3. *Father, restore communication, intimacy, and unity between me and my spouse, in Jesus' name.*
4. *Father, deliver us from every influence of unfaithfulness, suspicion, or neglect, in Jesus' name.*
5. *Lord, pour Your love afresh into our hearts and help us forgive as You forgave us, in Jesus' name.*
6. *I declare: My marriage will not die—by God's grace, we will love again, in Jesus' name*

*Tomorrow is the **ANNUAL PRAYER AND FASTING** program – **PRAYER STORM PRAYER DAY 2025.** Join us!*
*Theme: **ANOTHER LEVEL***
Contact: +237 681722404 or 695722340 for any inquiries.

Read: Luke 4:1–14;
       Exodus 3:1–10

      Bible in 1 year: Ps. 91-93
        Bible in 2 years: Mal. 3-4

"Behold, I am doing a new thing; now it springs forth, do you not perceive it? I will make a way in the wilderness and rivers in the desert" (Isaiah 43:19).

Welcome to the Annual Day of Prayer and Fasting for Prayer Storm.

This is a defining moment in our journey with God. He is calling us to ascend and embrace a new level. What God is talking about is more than growth in numbers or activity; it's a call to deeper obedience, greater consecration, and higher spiritual authority.

    For Christian Restoration Network (CRN), the year 2025 has been marked by undeniable evidence of God's hand – miracles, salvations, and restoration have spread across the nations. Yet now, through a prophetic Word, God declares: "It's time to rise. I'm doing something new."

    What does a new level mean? It's not about doing more for God but becoming more in Him. Jesus emerged from the wilderness *"in the power of the Spirit (Luke 4:14).* That was a shift into a new dimension. Moses stood before the burning bush and was thrust into destiny (Exodus 3). Paul relentlessly pursued his upward calling in Christ (Philippians 3:14), showing us that new levels require new depths.

God often prepares us through seasons that seem hidden – wildernesses, deserts, delays, but they are divine classrooms. Preparation precedes promotion. The wilderness refines. The secret place equips. The Word strengthens.

So how should we respond to the announcement of a new level? We must humble ourselves. We press in through prayer and fasting. We let go of what's comfortable and embrace what's next. We align with God's vision, trust His timing, and step forward by faith.

For CRN, a new level means greater reach, more profound impact, and a stronger prophetic voice to the nations. God is making rivers in the desert. The new has begun, do you perceive it?

Join us today to pray that God's plan for CRN will become a reality. Also, trust God for a brand-new beginning in your life.

Join Pastor Godson at 5 p.m. (GMT +1) for a time of prayer on YouTube/ Facebook. Infoline: (+237) 696 565 864/ 652 382 693 [SEND YOUR SUPPORT FOR FREE DISTRIBUTION OF BOOKS TO THIS NUMBERS]

Let us pray

1. *Thank You, Lord, for the ministry of Christian Restoration Network (CRN) and the global impact it has made in lives across the nations.*
2. *Thank You for Your consistent provision and supernatural supply in every season.*
3. *Thank You for preserving Pastor Godson and his team with divine protection and wisdom.*

4. *Father, we give You glory for the mighty works You have done through CRN in 2025.*
5. *Lord, prepare our hearts and minds to ascend to the next level of divine assignment.*
6. *Cleanse us from every distraction and help us to focus fully on Your calling.*
7. *Let there be a fresh outpouring of the Holy Spirit upon CRN and all its partners.*
8. *Open doors to new territories, nations, and communities that need Your restoration power.*
9. *Grant Pastor Godson and his team fresh revelation and divine strategy for the next phase.*
10. *Raise new leaders, intercessors, and vision carriers to partner with the mission.*
11. *Let signs, wonders, and miracles accompany every outreach in this new season.*
12. *Break every limitation and opposition resisting the advancement of CRN.*
13. *Father, declare and establish CRN's place in 2026 as a voice of revival to the nations.*
14. *Release prophetic clarity and divine blueprints for the next level in 2026.*
15. *In 2026, let CRN enter into multiplied influence, abundant provision, and global expansion for Your glory.*
16. *Add topics*

Saturday 20 December **KNOCK THEM DOWN**

Read: Jeremiah 47:6-7

Bible in 1 year: Ps. 138-142
Bible in 2 years: Catch Up

"Why have your warriors fallen? They cannot stand, for the LORD has knocked them down" (Jeremiah 46:15 NLT).

The prophet Jeremiah declared God's judgment against nations that had exalted themselves in pride, idolatry, and oppression. Mighty warriors who once terrified others could not stand when the Lord rose against them. Egypt's champions fell (Jeremiah 46:15), the Philistines faced the relentless sword of the Lord (Jeremiah 47:6-7), and Elam was scattered to the four winds (Jeremiah 49:36). God even declared, *"I will set my throne in Elam… and I will destroy its king and officials" (Jeremiah 49:38).*

This shows us that no power, no king, no nation can resist the purposes of God. When He decides to "Knock down," there is no human defense. He humbles the proud, frustrates the oppressor, and breaks every force that stands against His people.

For believers today, this is both a warning and a comfort. It is a warning that pride, rebellion, and disobedience invite divine opposition. No matter how strong we think we are, we cannot stand when God withdraws His hand. Yet it is also a comfort, for the enemies that rise against us are not too strong for the Lord. As He fought for

Israel, so He fights for us. Paul reminds us, *"If God is for us, who can be against us?" (Romans 8:31).*

Pharaoh's armies drowned in the Red Sea not because Israel was strong, but because the Lord fought for them (Exodus 14:27-28). In the same way, when you face opposition too great for you, God Himself can knock down your adversaries.

Are you under attack right now? Stand in humility and obedience before the Lord. Trust Him as your defender. His sword cannot rest until His mission is complete. Every stronghold against you will fall, for the battle belongs to Him.

Let us pray

1. *Father, thank You because no power can stand against You, in Jesus' name.*
2. *Lord, fight for me and my family against every force of opposition, in Jesus' name.*
3. *O Lord, knock down every stronghold of pride, rebellion, and oppression in my life, in Jesus' name.*
4. *Father, arise, let those who conspire against my destiny scatter, in Jesus' name.*
5. *Father, establish Your throne and reign over every area of my life, in Jesus' name.*
6. *I declare: My enemies will fall; I will stand victorious because the Lord is fighting for me, in Jesus' name.*

Sunday 21 December　　　**ENCOURAGE ONE ANOTHER DAILY**

Read: Hebrews 3:12-15

> **Bible in 1 year:** Ps. 143-145
> **Bible in 2 years:** Catch Up

"By this everyone will know that you are my disciples, if you love one another" (John 13:35 NIV).

Perseverance in the faith does not grow in isolation; it thrives in an atmosphere of encouragement. Hebrews 3:13 instructs us, *"Encourage one another daily… so that none of you may be hardened by sin's deceitfulness."* When encouragement is absent, hearts become vulnerable to doubt, compromise, and spiritual weariness. But when spoken, encouragement acts as a weapon of spiritual warfare, breaking the lies of the enemy and strengthening weary souls.

Jesus is our most outstanding example. When His disciples stumbled, He did not abandon them; He restored them. After Peter's denial, Jesus gave him a fresh commission: *"Feed my sheep."* When Thomas doubted, Jesus invited him to touch His wounds. In each case, love triumphed over failure. As He declared in John 13:35, our love for one another becomes the most powerful testimony of true discipleship. The man of God, T. D Jakes, said, "I told my children, no matter how you messed up, come back home."

Families, churches, and communities need to cultivate this culture of encouragement. It begins with affirming effort, not just outcomes. It continues by choosing words that build rather than break. Criticism and harsh judgment may come easily, but encouragement requires intentionality. Speak life into one another – remind your children, spouse, or brethren that God is at work in them even when progress seems slow.

Even the strongest among us can grow weary. Elijah, after calling down fire on Mount Carmel, sat under a broom tree and prayed to die (1 Kings 19). What revived him? A gentle touch and a word of assurance from the angel of the Lord. Likewise, a simple act of encouragement – a kind word, a heartfelt prayer, or a shared Scripture, can reignite someone's perseverance.

Make encouragement your daily habit. Say, *"I'm proud of you," "God is with you,"* or *"I'm standing beside you."* These words carry eternal weight. They breathe hope, heal wounds, and remind us that we are never walking alone.

Let us pray
1. *Father, thank You for the people You've placed in my life to walk this journey of faith, in Jesus' name.*
2. *Father, help us create a culture of love, encouragement, and support in our family, in Jesus' name.*
3. *Father, let my words be filled with grace and truth to lift those who are weary, in Jesus' name.*
4. *O Lord, heal every wounded heart in my home and restore joy to those discouraged, in Jesus' name.*
5. *Father, raise encouragers in my family—those who strengthen others with words of life, in Jesus' name.*
6. *I declare that my family shall be a wellspring of love, strength, and hope to this generation, in Jesus' name!*

Monday 22 December   **DON'T END ON THE WAY**

Read: 1 Corinthians 10:1-10

> **Bible in 1 year:** Ps. 146-150
> **Bible in 2 years:** Catch Up

"Better is the end of a thing than its beginning" (Ecclesiastes 7:8).

It is possible to begin a journey with God, experience divine encounters, witness miracles, receive provision, and yet never reach the finish line. The Israelites saw the Red Sea part, were fed by manna from heaven, drank water from the rock (which Paul tells us was Christ Himself), and were led daily by God's manifest presence in a cloud and fire. Yet, the majority of them did not make it to the Promised Land. Why? Because they became careless in the wilderness and settled into disobedience, idolatry, and cravings for things God had forbidden.

Paul warns the Corinthian believers that these stories were recorded not just for history but for *our warning*. He urges us to examine ourselves so that we do not begin with fire and end in failure. Galatians 5:7 puts it plainly: *"You were running the race so well. Who has held you back from following the truth?"* The Christian life is a race and a journey. Starting well is commendable, but finishing well is essential. Hence, Ecclesiastes 7:8 says, *"Better is the end of a thing than its beginning."*

The Greek word for "Scattered" in 1 Corinthians 10:5 is *'Katastrōnnymi,'* meaning to lay prostrate or to be overthrown. These were people with divine promises, but

131

they fell because their hearts wandered. Let that not be your story, in Jesus' name. Stay hungry for God. Stay alert. Stay holy.

Imagine a marathon runner who runs the first half with excellence but gets distracted at a water station and never finishes. The crowd cheers at the beginning, but the reward is at the end. God is calling you to endure until the finish line, empowered by Christ, the Author and Finisher of your faith.

Let us pray

1. *Father, I thank You for starting this journey with me and for every encounter I've had with You along the way, in Jesus' name.*
2. *Father, please forgive me for every moment I've lost focus, grown complacent, or allowed sin to harden my heart, in Jesus' name.*
3. *O Lord, renew my hunger for righteousness, and help me to pursue You with endurance and integrity, in Jesus' name.*
4. *Father, keep me from spiritual distractions and worldly cravings that pull me away from Your purpose, in Jesus' name.*
5. *Father, strengthen my inner man so I don't faint halfway, but press forward with joy to the very end, in Jesus' name.*
6. *I declare that I will finish strong, complete my assignment, and not be cast away. I will see the promise fulfilled,* **in Jesus' name.**

Prophetic Prayers of the Week

1. *"If God is for us, who can be against us?"* (Rom. 8:31); *No attack prevails against my family, in Jesus' name.*
2. *"The house of the righteous shall stand"* (Prov. 12:7); *My marriage will stand firm against any storm, in Jesus' name.*
3. *"You shall expand to the right and left"* (Isa. 54:3); *I will expand in all directions supernaturally in this land, in Jesus' name.*

Tuesday 23 December   **DECIDE TO GO**
                            THROUGH
Read: Romans 5:1-5

Bible in 1 year: Ps. 119
Bible in 2 years: Catch Up

"But he who stands firm to the end will be saved"
(Matthew 24:13 NIV).

God's process is rarely comfortable, but it is always purposeful and fruitful. Romans 5:3-4 teaches, *"We rejoice in our sufferings, because we know that suffering produces perseverance; perseverance, character; and character, hope."* Every trial becomes part of God's training ground, shaping those who are called to carry generational blessings.

The Greek word for *"Perseverance"* is *'hypomonē,'* meaning steadfast endurance, the ability to remain under pressure without breaking. It is not passive resignation, but active faith that refuses to quit until God's promise is fulfilled.

In my early ministry years, hardship was my constant companion. I often wept in secret, wondering if God had forgotten me. During one of my most painful seasons at Bible school, I had a dream. I saw people trying to harvest fruits from a mango tree before they were ripe. A voice said, *"Wait. Don't harvest yet. When they are ripe, shake the tree and gather all you want."* When I awoke, God whispered, *"Your beginning will be hard, but your end will be glorious."* That word anchored me through storms and delays.

Jesus Himself modeled this endurance. Hebrews 12:2 reminds us that He *"endured the cross, scorning its shame, for the joy set before Him."* He fixed His eyes not on the agony of the moment but on the glory of the outcome. In the same way, when the process hurts, don't let discouragement drive you off course. God doesn't rush what He is building to last. Endurance is not about escaping pain; it is about remaining faithful in the midst of it.

Your tears are not wasted. Every trial is producing strength, every delay is preparing a harvest, and every painful process is moving you closer to glory. Hold on; God is not finished with you yet.

Let us pray

1. *Father, thank You for Your faithfulness, even in my most painful seasons, in Jesus' name.*
2. *Lord, teach me to see the value in the process and to trust You in every stage, in Jesus' name.*
3. *Father, strengthen my heart when I grow weary or discouraged, in Jesus' name.*
4. *Father, help me remember that what You're building through me will bless generations, in Jesus' name.*
5. *Father, let my life and family testify that obedience through pain brings glorious reward, in Jesus' name.*
6. *I declare that no pain, delay, or trial shall derail my family's destiny; we will finish well, in Jesus' name!*

Wednesday 24 December   **BAPTIZED WITH**
                              FIRE

Read: Malachi 3:1-5; Luke 24:49

> **Bible in 1 year:** Gen. 1-2
> **Bible in 2 years:** Catch Up

"He will baptize you with the Holy Spirit and fire" (Matthew 3:11).

God wants to baptize you with fire so that you can be purified and equipped to live for Him and become a vessel of honor for His glory. If you desire to be a man or woman of impact in the Kingdom, you must be baptized with fire.

John the Baptist declared a profound truth about the ministry of Jesus: *"He will baptize you with the Holy Spirit and fire."* This baptism is not simply an outward ritual but an inward immersion in God's purifying and empowering presence.

The word baptize (*Baptizō* in Greek) means to immerse, to overwhelm, to submerge. To be baptized with fire means to be plunged into the burning presence of God until every part of your being is touched. Fire in Scripture purifies, refines, and consumes impurities, like a refiner's fire for silver and gold (Malachi 3:2-3). It also empowers – igniting zeal, passion, and boldness for God's mission.

When the Holy Spirit came on the Day of Pentecost, the Disciples were not just filled but transformed. Fear gave way to courage, silence turned into proclamation, and ordinary men became fiery witnesses who shook nations. That is the effect of being baptized with fire.

This baptism is not optional; it is essential for living the Christian life. Without fire, faith grows cold, prayer becomes mechanical, and witness becomes weak. But when the Spirit's fire burns within us, prayer becomes fervent, worship becomes alive, and witness becomes unstoppable.

John Wesley once said, "If you are on fire for God, people will come from miles to watch you burn." A life baptized in fire draws others to Christ because it radiates His passion and purity. Are you on fire for Jesus? If not, ask for the fire now!

Let us pray

1. *Father, thank You for the promise of baptism with the Holy Spirit and fire, in Jesus' name.*

2. *Father, please, immerse me fully in Your purifying fire, in Jesus' name.*

3. *Father, burn away every impurity, fear, and distraction in my life, in Jesus' name.*

4. *O Lord, ignite in us a fresh passion for prayer, worship, and service, in Jesus' name.*

5. *Father, empower me to be a bold and fiery witness of Christ, in Jesus' name.*

6. *I declare that I am baptized with fire and burning brightly for Jesus; I will see supernatural results this month, in Jesus' name.*

Thursday 25 December   **TRUE FREEDOM IN**
                               CHRIST

Read: Galatians 5:1-16

Bible in 1 year: Gen. 3-5
Bible in 2 years: Catch Up

"So, if the Son sets you free, you will be free indeed" (John 8:36).

Freedom is not simply the absence of visible chains. True freedom is deeper; it is the dominion over self, anxiety, fear, and sin. You are truly free when pleasing God becomes your highest pursuit, when selfish ambition no longer dictates your choices, and when the weight of people's opinions no longer enslaves your heart.

The path of freedom with God can be lonely. Jesus said, *"Enter by the narrow gate" (Matthew 7:13-14).* Freedom means walking away from the broad road of compromise, even if it leaves you misunderstood or isolated. Yet in that narrow path lies joy, peace, and eternal reward.

Freedom begins with surrender. Paul declared, *"I have been crucified with Christ, and I no longer live, but Christ lives in me" (Galatians 2:20).* When you die to self, you rise into the liberty of Christ. No law, demon, or fear can dominate a life fully yielded to God.

Anxiety, fear, and selfish pursuits are inner prisons. Christ, through His Spirit, gives us dominion over these inner tyrants. The Greek word for freedom, *'Eleutheria,'* carries the sense of release with authority. It is not aimless liberty but purposeful living under God's reign.

Beloved, freedom is not about how much you can do, but about who you now belong to. In Christ, you are free to obey, free to love, and free to walk in holiness. This freedom is not popular and may sometimes feel lonely, but it is glorious and eternal.

Let us pray

1. *Father, thank You for setting me free from sin and fear, in Jesus' name.*
2. *Father, deliver me from every hidden chain of anxiety and selfish ambition, in Jesus' name.*
3. *Holy Spirit, empower me to walk daily in the dominion of Christ, in Jesus' name.*
4. *Lord, grant me courage to walk the lonely path of freedom with You, in Jesus' name.*
5. *I declare that I am free indeed, living to please God alone, in Jesus' name.*
6. *I am free and married to Jesus Christ; Satan shall never put a yoke on me again, in Jesus' name.*

Friday 26 December

FRUITFULNESS: YOUR COVENANT RIGHT

Read: John 15:5-8;
Psalm 127:3-5

Bible in 1 year: Gen. 6-9
Bible in 2 years: Catch Up

"Then God blessed them, and God said to them, 'Be fruitful and multiply; fill the earth and subdue it; have dominion...'" (Genesis 1:28).

The very first words God spoke to humanity were not warnings, corrections, or conditions; they were a blessing. This is a foundational truth that breaks every false belief of inferiority or limitation. You were not born under a curse but created under a covenant. Genesis 1:28 is more than a historical declaration; it is an ongoing spiritual reality in Christ: YOU ARE BLESSED TO BE FRUITFUL.

Fruitfulness in Scripture goes far beyond biological reproduction. It speaks of growth, productivity, effectiveness, multiplication, and lasting impact. The Hebrew word *'Parah'* means "To increase with purpose." God designed you to produce meaningful results, not to be busy, but to be effective. Jesus confirmed this in John 15:5: *"He who abides in Me...bears much fruit."* Your fruitfulness flows, not from striving, but from abiding in Him.

I remember visiting my spiritual father a few years ago to honor him. He prayed for me with deep passion, and I felt as though a divine garment covered me. I left carrying

139

something I could not fully explain. When I got to my wife, I was trembling, quietly praying in tongues, repeating, "Something has happened to me today." My wife, surprised by my state, asked what was wrong. I shared my encounter, and though I had prayed with many anointed men of God, this impartation was unlike any other. From that day, my life and ministry shifted to a higher level. That was not a coincidence; it was a covenant blessing in action.

God's command to "Have dominion" (*radah*) means to reign with spiritual authority, not by controlling people, but by governing your God-given space under His guidance. This is your inheritance. Reject small thinking, refuse survival, and embrace your covenant right to supernatural increase. The blessing that spoke in the beginning is still speaking over you today. You are blessed in Jesus' name!

Let us pray
1. *Father, thank You for blessing me with fruitfulness from the very beginning and calling me to be productive and influential, in Jesus' name.*
2. *Lord, help me walk in the full authority of the Genesis Blessing and be fruitful in every area of my life, in Jesus' name.*
3. *I reject every mentality of barrenness and stagnation and receive the grace to multiply and advance, in Jesus' name.*
4. *Let everything in my life – ministry, family, business, and career, bear lasting fruit, in Jesus' name.*
5. *Father, teach me to be a faithful steward of Your blessings in my life, in Jesus' name.*
6. *I declare that I am fruitful, and I will multiply and fill spaces, subdue opposition, and reign with purpose, in Jesus' name.*

Saturday 27 December

CONFESS AND BE FREE

Read: James 5:14-16

> **Bible in 1 year:** Gen. 10-11
> **Bible in 2 years:** Catch Up

"If we confess our sins, He is faithful and just to forgive us our sins and to cleanse us from all unrighteousness" *(1 John 1:9).*

Confession is not bondage; it is freedom. Sin thrives in secrecy. What is hidden in darkness gains power over us, but once brought into the light through confession, its grip is broken. Confession to God brings forgiveness, while confession to others opens the door to healing. Both are vital for complete freedom.

The Greek word for "Confess" is *'Homologeō,'* which means "To say the same thing, to agree." In confession, we agree with God about the seriousness of sin instead of excusing or minimizing it. By admitting the truth, we position ourselves to receive His mercy and cleansing.

David discovered this truth after hiding his sin: *"When I kept silent, my bones wasted away... Then I acknowledged my sin to You... and You forgave" (Psalm 32:3-5).* Silence brought torment, but confession brought freedom.

Confession to others is equally powerful. James 5:16 teaches us to confess to one another so that we may be healed. This is not about telling everyone, but sharing with trusted, mature believers who can pray with us, encourage us, and hold us accountable. A man carrying a heavy bag for a long distance becomes exhausted. But when he finally sets it down, he feels light and free. Confession is like laying down a burden; you no longer carry it alone.

The freedom of confession is not in shame but in release. God longs to lift the weight of guilt and replace it with the joy of His forgiveness. True freedom is found in honesty before Him and accountability with others. Confess your sins today and be free!

Let us pray

1. *Father, thank You for the freedom that comes through confession, in Jesus' name.*
2. *O Lord, help me to agree with You about my sins without excuses, in Jesus' name.*
3. *Father, release me from every hidden burden I have carried, in Jesus' name.*
4. *Give me courage to seek accountability where needed, in Jesus' name.*
5. *Restore my joy and fill me with Your peace, in Jesus' name.*

Sunday 28 December   **GOD EXPOSES SIN TO HEAL**

Read: 2 Samuel 12:1-13

> **Bible in 1 year:** Gen. 12-15
> **Bible in 2 years:** Catch Up

"He who covers his sins will not prosper, but whoever confesses and forsakes them will have mercy" (Proverbs 28:13).

God sometimes exposes our sins – either privately in our conscience or publicly through others. His goal is never to shame us but to heal, deliver, and restore us. Sin blinds, deceives, and destroys. If left unchecked, it grows like a disease that consumes life. Exposure is God's mercy at work.

When Nathan confronted David about his sin with Bathsheba, it was a painful but necessary moment. David's repentance (Psalm 51) was sincere and profound. The Greek word for repentance, *'Metanoia,'* means "A change of mind that results in a change of direction." It is more than remorse or regret; it is sorrow for choosing our way instead of God's way, followed by turning back to Him. Remorse weeps because it got caught; repentance weeps because it grieved God.

Confession has two parts. First, confession to God brings forgiveness: *"If we confess our sins, He is faithful and just to forgive" (1 John 1:9).* Because Christ died for us, there is no sin too deep for God's pardon. He casts confessed sins as far as the east is from the west (Psalm 103:12) and remembers them no more (Isaiah 43:25).

Second, confession to others brings healing: *"Confess your sins to one another… that you may be healed" (James 5:16).* This requires humility and courage, and it should be done wisely – with trusted, mature believers. Forgiveness comes from God, but healing often flows through accountability and community.

A wound left hidden festers, but when exposed and cleaned, it heals. In the same way, God exposes sin not to destroy us but to heal us. Cooperate with Him for your deliverance.

Let us pray

1. *Father, thank You for exposing sin to heal me, in Jesus' name.*
2. *Lord, give me true repentance, not mere remorse, in Jesus' name.*
3. *Father, forgive and cleanse me from all hidden faults, in Jesus' name.*
4. *O Father, grant me courage to confess wisely and walk in healing, in Jesus' name.*
5. *Father, as I confess and abandon sin, please restore my joy and fellowship with You, in Jesus' name.*
6. *I refuse to cover the sin God has exposed in my life, in Jesus' name.*

TOUCH AND
                                 TRANSFER

Read: Mark 10:13-16

Bible in 1 year: Gen. 16-19
Bible in 2 years: Catch Up

"Now Joshua son of Nun was filled with the spirit of wisdom because Moses had laid his hands on him. So, the Israelites listened to him and did what the Lord had commanded Moses" (Deuteronomy 34:9).

There is a spiritual transaction that occurs when a blessing is released, and it is not limited to words; it also flows through touch. Throughout Scripture, the laying on of hands has been a divine channel for transferring power, activating purpose, and releasing blessing. When Jesus blessed the children in Mark 10:16, He did not merely speak a prayer; He laid His hands on them. That moment was not symbolic; it was supernatural. In the same way, when Jacob placed his hands on Ephraim and Manasseh, destinies were reshaped in alignment with God's plan (Genesis 48).

Touch, combined with prophetic declaration, releases supernatural results. Parents who intentionally bless their children through words and touch embed identity, vision, and destiny within them. Not long ago, I asked the parents in our church to lay hands on their children and bless them every day for seven days. By the end of that period, we witnessed remarkable testimonies. Children experienced healing, and academic breakthroughs were recorded; even stubborn and difficult cases were completely transformed.

This practice is not reserved for parents alone. Every believer carries the Spirit of God, and that same Spirit that anointed Jesus for miracles (Acts 10:38) flows through your touch when exercised by faith. The Greek word 'Epitithēmi,' translated "Lay" in Mark 10:16, means to impose, apply, or transfer. It is the same word used when the apostles laid hands to heal the sick or impart the Holy Spirit (Acts 6:6; Acts 8:17). This reveals that laying on of hands is not a tradition; it is transmission. When Moses laid hands on Joshua, wisdom and empowerment were released (Deuteronomy 34:9).

One father who had struggled to connect with his teenage daughter once laid hands on her and spoke prophetic words. She wept, saying, "That's the first time I've ever heard you believe in me." That single moment shifted her spiritual journey forever.

Let us pray

1. *Father, thank You for giving me the power to bless through both my words and my hands, in Jesus' name.*
2. *Lord, make me a vessel anointed to release identity, peace, healing, and destiny to others, in Jesus' name.*
3. *Father, let every impartation I release carry divine weight, accuracy, and supernatural backing, in Jesus' name.*
4. *Father, heal broken family relationships and restore generational blessings through intentional spiritual acts, in Jesus' name.*
5. *Father, use my hands as instruments of healing, affirmation, and restoration, and let every touch carry the oil of the Spirit, in Jesus' name.*
6. *I declare that I am a carrier of blessing; when I lay hands, heaven releases virtue, and my touch brings healing, restoration, affirmation, and activation, in Jesus' name.*

Prophetic Prayers of the Week

1. *"The angel rolled away the stone"* (Matt. 28:2); *Every barrier before me this week is rolled away, in Jesus' name.*
2. *"The Lord remembered Hannah"* (1 Sam. 1:19); *The Lord will remember me this week and favor me, in Jesus' name.*
3. *"Let justice roll like a river"* (Amos 5:24); *Justice prevails in my nation, in Jesus' name.*

Tuesday 30 December **THE GOD OF SECOND CHANCES**

Read: 2 Samuel 12:1-13

> **Bible in 1 year:** Gen. 20-22
> **Bible in 2 years:** Catch Up

"The steadfast love of the LORD never ceases; His mercies never come to an end; they are new every morning; great is Your faithfulness" (Lamentations 3:22-23).

Have you fallen and felt like God has completely turned His back on you? Today, His mercy has found you. He is offering you a second chance – don't miss it, receive it now!

David's failure was monumental, yet God's mercy gave him another chance. Though consequences remained, his life was not discarded. Instead, God continued to use him, and from his line came Solomon, and ultimately Jesus Christ, the Savior of the world. This is the testimony of the God of second chances.

The Hebrew word for mercy *(Chesed)* speaks of God's covenant love – loyal, unfailing, and undeserved. It is this mercy that gives us new beginnings when we deserve judgment.

Every saint in Scripture had moments of failure: Moses struck the rock, Peter denied Jesus, Jonah ran away from God. Yet in each case, God gave another opportunity. Failure is never final with Him. Consider a potter! After a vessel is marred in his hands, he does not throw away the clay. Instead, he reshapes it into another vessel as it pleases him (Jeremiah 18:4). So, it is with God; He refashions broken lives for His glory.

The God of second chances does not just forgive; He restores, recommissions, and reuses. His grace will make your story a testimony that failure is not the end, but a setup for a greater divine purpose.

Let us pray

1. *Father, thank You for being the God of second chances, in Jesus' name.*
2. *O Father, rewrite my story with Your mercy and grace, in Jesus' name.*
3. *Father, please, restore every area of my life where I have failed You, in Jesus' name.*
4. *Father, use my brokenness as a vessel for Your glory, in Jesus' name.*
5. *Father, keep me standing in Your mercy and purpose, in Jesus' name.*
6. *I consecrate myself to God's use; Satan will no longer use me, in Jesus' name.*

Wednesday 31 December **AT THE DOOR OF**
BREAKTHROUGH

Read: Genesis 41:39-41

> **Bible in 1 year:** Gen. 23-26
> **Bible in 2 years:** Catch Up

"And the God of all grace, who called you to his eternal glory in Christ, after you have suffered a little while, will himself restore you and make you strong, firm and steadfast" (1 Peter 5:10).

When God is about to give you something big, He first prepares you to handle it. Blessings from God are weighty; without preparation, they can overwhelm, corrupt, or be wasted. Divine preparation is often hidden in seasons of trials, pruning, and testing.

Joseph is a clear example. Before he wore Pharaoh's ring, he wore chains in prison. Betrayal by his brother, slavery in Potiphar's house, and false accusations were painful, but each step developed humility, wisdom, and resilience in him. At the appointed time, God elevated him suddenly, but the years of preparation ensured he would not waste the blessing (Genesis 41:39-41).

David's story echoes the same truth. Anointed as king while still a shepherd, he faced lions and bears before confronting Goliath. Later, years of running from Saul tested his patience and forged his character. By the time he ascended the throne, David was not only a warrior but a man after God's heart (1 Samuel 17:34-37; Acts 13:22).

Even Jesus embraced preparation. Before His public ministry, the Spirit led Him into the wilderness for

150

forty days of testing (Matthew 4:1-11). That season of spiritual battle confirmed His readiness for the mission ahead.

When God is about to give you something big, you may notice:

1. **Unusual testing** – challenges that stretch your faith (James 1:2-4).
2. **Closed doors** – divine delays that protect you until the right moment (Revelation 3:7).
3. **Pruning** – God removes people or habits that hinder your growth (John 15:2).
4. **Deepened hunger for God** – prayer and the Word become essential, preparing you to steward greater responsibility (Psalm 42:1-2).

Beloved, if you are currently going through a tough trial, don't despise it. Big blessings require big preparation. Endure with faith, for the God who called you will restore, strengthen, and establish you in due time, in Jesus' name (1 Peter 5:10).

Let us pray

1. *Father, I thank You because every trial is preparing me for greater glory, in Jesus' name.*
2. *Lord, give me patience to endure seasons of waiting without murmuring, in Jesus' name.*
3. *Father, prune every relationship, habit, or distraction that would hinder my promotion, in Jesus' name.*
4. *Lord, strengthen me to grow in character, wisdom, and faith as I await my breakthrough, in Jesus' name.*
5. *Father, open my eyes to recognize small opportunities that lead to big blessings, in Jesus' name.*

6. *I declare that I am prepared, equipped, and ready to step into the big blessing God has ordained for me, in Jesus' name.*

WHAT YOUR SUPPORT WILL DO

It is very clear through the numerous miracles, breakthroughs and transformation of lives that God has chosen to use this ministry to stir a revival among His people in Cameroon and beyond. I received the call alone but I cannot execute it alone. You have a unique role to play in this divine project. Join us as we take the Gospel to every corner of Cameroon and beyond.

We want to start placing copies of this book in hotels, hospitals, schools and homes, to touch the lives of people with the gospel of Jesus Christ. Just as you have been blessed by this book, they too will be mightily blessed.

TESTIMONY

Every month, hundreds of copies of this Prayer Storm Daily Prayer Guide are distributed freely, thanks to the kind gesture of our partners. May God bless all of you who faithfully sponsor this outreach through your financial seed. You too can sponsor 10, 25, 50, 100 or even more copies to be printed and distributed charge-free to those who are hungry for the word.

Call the numbers: (237) 699.90.26.18 or 674.49.58.95 send an email to voiceofrevivalcameroon@yahoo.com.

If you want to become a distributor of our literature, contact us directly and we will give you the directives on how to do so.

WHERE TO BUY THIS PRAYER GUIDE

CRN Centres

- **Yaounde:** *Prayer Storm Headquarters:* 1st Floor Storey Building at Entrée Lycée de Tsinga village on the edge of the main road. **Contact:** 681.72.24.04/ 696.56.58.64

- **Bamenda:** Revival Christian Book Center, **Cow Street**: 675.14.04.50/ 694.20.04.51

- **Douala/PK 8:** All American Depot opposite Lycée **Cité des Palmiers**: 678.04.11.41/ 696.90.76.09/ 670.34.42.32

Adamawa

- **Banyo:** FGM: 677.92.05.98/ 674.64.71.31
- **Meinganga:** EEL: 699.65.02.67/ 652.70.40.68
- **Ngaoundere:** EEC Mont des Oliviers: 674.14.20.51, EEL: 690.06.37.14
- **Tibati:** EEC: 681.01.33.34

Centre

- **Eseka:** FGM: 675.07.56.24
- **Mbalmayo:** EEC: 675.12.86.85/
- **Mfou:** FGM: 677.36.43.28
- **Monatelé:** FGM: 677.58.42.99
- **Yaounde:** EEC **Biyem-assi**: 675.61.86.00/ 677.49.95.83/ 691.26.18.08, EEC **Nlongkak**: 677.56.41.09, EEC **Nouvelle Alliance**: 670.80.56.93, FGM **Biyem-assi**: 675.14.72.70, FGM **Etoug-Ebé**: 671.47.75.78/ 673.50.42.33, Galaxy Computers, Châteaux **Ngoa-Ekelle**: 670.52.75.26, **Yaounde: Librairie Chrétienne** Les Champions op. Total Caveau, **Mvog-Ada**: 675.51.02.86, **LC Maison de la Grâce**, Montée Jouvence op. Olympia: 675.38.46.96, **LC Maison de la Bénédiction**, Marché

Nsam: 691.64.47.84, **LC la Rhema**, Marché Essos, Terminus: 679.39.37.42, **LC Maison du Salut**, Pharmacie du Soleil, Carrefour MEEC: 674.85.16.33/ 699.33.85.11, **LC Livre de Vie**, Mini ferme: 675.00.45.60, **LC Bethesda**, Tsinga: 679.97.06.26, **Overcomers Christian Bookshop**, op. Djongolo Hospital, EtoaMeki: 677.16.46.20, **Mount Zion Christian Bookshop**, op. SONEL TKC: 663.25.86.23 / 675.21.94.35, **Tongolo**: 675.62.86.00, **Olembe**: 651.63.52.34, **DGI-Carrefour Abbia** 652.22.22.49, **Messassi**: 675.24.70.73, **Nkozoa**: 670.29.50.18, **Essos**: 677.53.94.52, **Odzja**: 679.97.47.08, **Etoug-Ebé**: 675.37.18.11, **Mimboman**: 699.90.52.84, **Poste Centrale**: 650.70.08.07, **Emombo**: 699.90.52.84, **Lycée Emana**: 677.86.23.14

East

- **Batouri:** FGM: 664.86.41.80
- **Bertoua:** CBC, **quartier Ngaikada** ou **Aprilé centrale** sous-préfecture: 678.00.63.20/ 694.25.69.20, Collège Bilingue de l'Orient, entrée Hôpital Régionale, **quartier Italy**: 670.56.81.49, FGM, **Nkolbikon**: 696.57.95.43, 677.65.46.76, FGM, **Tigaza**: 674.15.13.18
- **Yokadouma:** FGM: 673.16.24.95/ 696.51.73.70

Far-North

- **Maroua:** Église Missionnaire du Réveil (EMIR) **Baoliwop**: 694.43.33.63, FGM **Harde**: 675.33.12.27, Roman Catholic Church: 673.15.19.76
- **Yagoua:** FGM: 675.691.869

Littoral

Douala: Dakar: La Gloire Phone, immeuble X Tigi, Commissariat 11e: 697.60.57.85, **Kotto:** Behind Neptune fuel station, **Bloc M:** 677.68.18.52, **Bonaberi:** 677.89.87.46, **Akwa:** 691.04.14.59/ 677.91.29.45, **Logpom:** 677.68.18.52/ 651.78.57.30**, Carrefour Lycée de Maképé:** 698.09.42.63, **PK 12 (Marché):** 677.91.29.45/ 696.13.99.26, **Texaco-Nkoulouluon:** 675.18.79.85/695112610 691.04.14.59, **Terminus Saint Michel :** 675187985, La Gloire Phone, Maison X. Tigi, **Carrefour entrée Bille:** 678.19.90.85, **PK 21:** 670.79.05.40/ 691.04.14.59, **Bonanjo:** 691.04.14.59, 677061705 691.04.14.59, **Ange Raphael ESSEC:** 694.26.12.28/ 677.91.29.45, 698360441, **Bonamoussadi Maetur:** 694.26.12.28/ 677.91.29.45, **Village:** 670.79.05.40/ 691.04.14.5, Sure Foundation **Bonabéri:** Ancienne route op. Lycée de Bonaberi Winners Chapel: 671.403.761

- **Nkongsamba:** FGM: 676.40.90.55
- **Melong - GCEPAL:** Tel: 677.80.16.45

North

- **Garoua:** FGM: 678.67.04.22/ 699.91.91.65

North-West

- **Bamenda:** Bamenda Main Market, **Shed 15**: 679.45.11.88, Carmel Cooperative Credit Union (CarCCUL), **Sonac Street**/Tél: 651.04.21.27, FGM NW1 Area office, opposite Garanti Express: 679.46.63.31, FGM, **Cow Street**: 677.21.97.22, FGM, **Mbomassa**: 683.40.40.88, Omega Fire Ministry, **Foncha junction**: 677.93.19.98, ACADI head office, **Wakiki junction**: 672.82.77.84, SUMAN Christian Book Center, **Sonac Street**: 675.72.91.32/ 665.49.98.48, Victory Computers, Food market, **Fishpond hill**: 677.64.19.54, Wailing Women: 696.00.35.07/ 674.57.36.76

- **Batibo:** FGM: 677.31.25.45
- **Njinikom/Mbingo:** BERUDA: 677.60.14.07
- **Jakiri:** FGM, **Nkar**: 677.73.82.91
- **Kumbo:** FGM: 675.72.91.32
- **Mbengwi:** FGM: 677.33.73.86
- **Ndop:** Bruno Bijouterie, Central park: 674.97.59.34
- **Wum:** FGM Central Town: 677.64.32.56, PCC Kesu: 677.13.83.51

West

- **Bafang:** FGM, **Bafang**: 655.00.25.57
- **Bafia:** FGM: 675.21.92.95/ 695.54.96.14
- **Bafoussam:** Alliance biblique du Cameroun, **Tamdja**, SOREPCO: 699.74.79.10, Radio Bonne Nouvelle: 699.93.09.32, Librairie chrétienne du **Camp** oignon: 699.51.47.25, LC PAROLE DE VIE, **gare routière de** Ndiangdam: 699.75.50.99, Dépôt RAYON AMBIANCE **marché A**: 699.42.78.47, EEC **Tamdja**: 696.14.90.16, EEC **Kamkop**: 699.44.03.59, EEC **Plateau**: 696.17.54.23, EEC **Toket**: 695.56.43.61, EEC **SOCADA**: 697.85.65.65, EEC **Tyo-Baleng**: 670.89.70.52, EEC **Kouogouo**: 675.42.27.86, EEC **Diangdam**: 698.35.20.37, FGM **Kamkop**: 653.83.11.80, Faith Bible Church: 683.94.01.21
- **Baham:** FGM: 677.47.55.79
- **Bandjoun:** FGM: 676.41.49.09
- **Bangangte:** EEC **Banekane**: 677.86.47.68
- **Banyo:** FGM: 677.92.05.98/ 674.64.71.31
- **Dschang:** FGM: 675.18.79.85/ 656.20.07.02, FGM **Minmeto**: 681.08.78.37/ 655.01.81.09

157

- **Foumban:** Décoration Splendeur, **CAMOCO**/Tel.: 677.79.30.83/ 694.85.09.25
- **Kombou:** EEC: 675.81.36.07
- **Mbouda:** FGM: 696.10.41.33/ 676.36.18.11, Cyber Café Pressing near Espace Saint Pierre du Fossie, op. Party House: 675.00.91.15, EEC **Mbouda Centre**: 695.61.97.79

South

- **Ebolowa:** FGM: 677.66.00.19/ 671.90.97.22
- **Kribi:** Carrefour Django: 675.957.912
- **Kye-Ossi:** FGM: 678.78.00.90/ 699.95.96.99

South-West

- **Buea:** FGM **Molyko**: 677.86.47.68, Molyko, near Express Union, **Check Point**: 675.06.37.78,
- **Ekona:** FGM: 675.84.26.91
- **Kumba:** Caisse Populaire Coopérative Carmel (CarCCUL), **Sonac Street**: 675.45.12.21, Glorious Christian Book Center, **Sonac Street**: 677.62.58.49
- **Lebialem:** FGM de **Talung**, Bamumbu – Wabane: 670.466.121
- **Limbe:** Librairie Amen, **New town**: 677.16.51.62, FGM **Mawoh**: 675.78.94.19, FGM **Cow Fence**: 675.73.20.02
- **Misaje:** Kingdom Restoration Parish (KRP) **opposite the hospital**: 679.33.66.53
- **Mutengene:** FGM: 675.36.36.84
- **Muyuka:** FGM: 673.428.985, Royal Priesthood Nursery and Primary School: 677.72.76.80
- **Tiko:** FGM: 654.88.75.57, 674.47.34.36
- **Tombel:** Baptist Church Waterfall: 677.92.33.58

ABROAD:

- **N'Djamena (Chad):** Evang. Kaltouma Aguidi: (235) 95.01.99.92
- **Libreville (Gabon):** Rev. Petipa Flaubert: (241) 05.31.27.39

Pay for your book orders (DISTRIBUTORS ONLY) at:
EcoBank, Acc. No: 0200212620638901 **or** ORANGE Mobile Money, Acc. No: 696880058
Info lines: (237) 677436964, 675686005, 673571953, 679465717;
crnprayerstorm@gmail.com,
prayerstorm@christianrestorationnetwork.org,
www.christianrestorationnetwork.org

Send Financial Support to: ECOBANK Bamenda Acc. No: 0040812604565101 **or** Carmel Cooperative Credit Union Ltd. Bamenda Acc. No: 261 **or** ORANGE Mobile Money: 699902618 **or** MTN Mobile Money: 674495895.

PUBLICATIONS BY CHRISTIAN RESTORATION NETWORK (CRN/PRAYER STORM)

1- Prayer Storm Daily Prayer Guide (monthly devotional)
2- Power Must Change Hands Vol.1: Dealing with Evil Foundations
3- Power Must Change Hands Vol.2: Pursue Overtake and Recover All
4- Power Must Change Hands Vol.3: Jesus Christ Must Reign
5- Power Must Change Hands Vol.4: Arise and Shine
6- Power Must Change Hands Vol.5: Family Restoration 1
7- Power Must Change Hands Vol.6: Family Restoration 2
8- Power Must Change Hands Vol.7: Raise an Altar
9- Power Must Change Hands Vol.8: Commanding Total Victory
10- Power Must Change Hands Vol.9: Enjoying Your Freedom in Christ
11- Power Must Change Hands Vol.10: Supernatural Breakthrough
12- Festival of Fire Series No.1: Let the Fire Fall
13- Festival of Fire Series No.2: Anointed Vessels
14- Festival of Fire Series No.3: God's Agent of Revival
15- Festival of Fire Series No.4: Raising Altars of Restoration
16- Festival of Fire Series No.5: Foundations of a Blessed Family
17- Dominion
18- Divine Overflow
19- Unbreakable

20- Higher Heights
21- Arresting Family Destroyers 1
22- Arresting Family Destroyers 2
23- Praying Like Jesus
24- Conquering the Giant Called Poverty
25- Generous Living
26- Bind the Strongman
27- Personal and Family Deliverance
28- A Difference by Fire
29- Your Time for Divine Expansion
30- Jesus Our Jubilee
31- The Choice of a Friend
32- Christians and Politics
33- A Dynamic Prayer Life
34- Restoring Broken Foundations

NB: Our publications are in English and French.

For copies, contact your local books store or direct your request to:

Prayer Storm Team
P.O. Box 5018 Nkwen, Bamenda
Tel.: (237) 679465717 or 675686005 or 677436964
crnprayerstorm@gmail.com
prayerstorm@christianrestorationnetwork.org

Prayer Storm Online Store:
With MTN or Orange Mobile Money *(for those in Cameroon)* and E-Wallet *(for those abroad)*, you can easily obtain the electronic version of this book and other CRN publications via **www.amazon.com** or via **www.amazon.com** at

https://shorturl.at/pqxyT or
www.christianrestorationnetwork.org/our-bookstore.
https://goo.gl/ktf3rT

Contact (237) 679.46.57.17 or
prayerstorm@christianrestorationnetwork.org